BACKABLE

BACKABLE

THE SURPRISING TRUTH BEHIND WHAT
MAKES PEOPLE TAKE A CHANCE ON YOU

SUNEEL GUPTA
WITH CARLYE ADLER

Little, Brown and Company

New York Boston London

Little, Brown and Company
Hachette Book Group
1290 Avenue of the Americas, New York, NY 10104
littlebrown.com

First Edition: February 2021

Little, Brown and Company is a division of Hachette Book Group, Inc. The Little, Brown name and logo are trademarks of Hachette Book Group, Inc.

The publisher is not responsible for websites (or their content) that are not owned by the publisher.

The Hachette Speakers Bureau provides a wide range of authors for speaking events. To find out more, go to hachettespeakersbureau.com or call (866) 376-6591.

ISBN 978-0-316-49451-9 (hardcover) / 978-0-316-20473-6 (international edition)
LCCN 2020943057

Printing 1, 2020

LSC-C

Printed in the United States of America

To Mom, who taught me how to wonder.
And to Leena, who showed me how to believe.

CONTENTS

AUTHOR'S NOTE   *3*

INTRODUCTION   *5*

STEP 1: CONVINCE YOURSELF FIRST   **15**
Schedule Incubation Time   18
Steer into Objections   24
Throwaway Work   28
Measure Your Emotional Runway   30

STEP 2: CAST A CENTRAL CHARACTER   **33**
Choose One Person   35
Create a Storyboard   39
Keep Your Character in Sight   43

STEP 3: FIND AN EARNED SECRET   **48**
Go Beyond Google   51
Intoxicate Them with Effort   54

STEP 4: MAKE IT FEEL INEVITABLE   **61**
Be an Armchair Anthropologist   62
With or Without Us   66
Show Momentum   70
Have Vision, Not Visions   71

STEP 5: FLIP OUTSIDERS TO INSIDERS   75

Share What It Could Be, Not How It Has to Be   78

The Story of Us   82

Make *Them* the Hero   85

Share Just Enough   89

STEP 6: PLAY EXHIBITION MATCHES   94

No Venue Is Too Small   97

Be Willing to Be Embarrassed   100

Don't Ask, "What Do You Think?"   101

Build Your Backable Circle   104

The Rule of 21   109

Reboot Your Style   111

STEP 7: LET GO OF YOUR EGO   114

Show, Don't Tell   115

Forget Yourself   117

Find the Passionate Few   121

CONCLUSION: THE GAME OF NOW   127

ACKNOWLEDGMENTS   135

APPENDIX 1: Chapter Summaries   137

*APPENDIX 2: Highlights from Select Interviews
with Backable People*   147

    Kirsten Green   148

    Peter Chernin   155

    Adam Lowry   166

    Tina Sharkey   174

    Andy Dunn   183

    Brian Grazer   192

CONTENTS

Ann Miura-Ko   200

Trevor McFedries   207

John Palfrey   213

NOTES   *219*

INDEX   *233*

BACKABLE

AUTHOR'S NOTE

Years of learning went into this book and some conversations have been retold to the best of my memory. In order to protect the privacy of certain individuals, a few names and identifying characteristics have been changed.

INTRODUCTION

I wanted to bail, but it was too late. In a few moments, I'd be telling a story to a packed house of Silicon Valley overachievers. It was a cautionary tale of a career that had gone off the rails through canceled projects, missed promotions, and near-bankrupt startups. It was ugly, but also entertaining. So why was I having second thoughts? Because this story was my own.

A few weeks earlier I'd received a call from a restricted number. I answered it, hoping it was one of the many investors who hadn't gotten back to me. But instead the person introduced herself as the organizer of an event called FailCon, which stands for Failure Conference. "It's funny," she said. "You've been nominated twice to speak at our conference." Funny to her, maybe, but I wasn't laughing. I deepened my voice as much as a little Indian guy can and tried to express my credibility as a professional and an entrepreneur.

I told her about my new startup idea. Rise was a telehealth

service that matched you with a personal nutritionist right over your mobile phone. What I didn't tell her is that it wasn't going very well. I hadn't been able to recruit people to join me or find investors to fund the idea. She seemed to intuitively pick up on my desperation and mentioned that there might be investors in the audience. That's all I needed to hear. I agreed right then and there to be the keynote speaker for FailCon.

Moments before my speech I began to question my life choices. How did things turn out this way? I grew up in sub-urban Michigan, finished college there, and took an IT job in downtown Detroit. The pay was decent, but each day was the same as the last, troubleshooting issues, building spreadsheets, and maintaining databases. It was simple, mind-numbing work. I was waiting for someone to point in my direction and say, "That kid's a star! Let's find a better way to make use of his talents." That didn't happen. In a sea of cubicles, I sat at my desk waiting to be discovered.

Eventually, I did what some people do when they feel directionless—I went to law school. In my third year, I re-ceived a job offer from a chest-thumping corporate firm based in Midtown Manhattan. The signing bonus itself was twice the salary I was earning in Detroit. But I got a sinking feeling that taking the job would send me back to the same headspace I was in three years earlier...restless and bored. I might not have known exactly what I was looking for, but I knew this wasn't it.

So I turned down the offer and began cold-calling people in Silicon Valley. I wanted to be part of a company that was building something, creating something. I eventually landed a job at Mozilla, the maker of Firefox. I was supposed to be working on legal matters, but I found myself drawn to the other side of the building, where the engineers and designers sat. I'd peek over their shoulders and ask if I could help with anything, no matter how small. Eventually, they gave me the chance to lead and launch a new product feature for Firefox. Collaborating with those engineers and designers to create something new fueled a fire in me. I had finally found what I was meant to do.

What I learned at Mozilla taught me enough to be recruited to a little-known startup as its first head of product development. That startup grew into Groupon. Within two years, we employed more than ten thousand people around the globe. We were making hundreds of millions of dollars a year. We were growing faster than Google, faster than Facebook, faster than Apple. A *Forbes* magazine cover named Groupon the "fastest growing company...ever." The company went public in the largest IPO by a US internet company since Google.[1]

Then it all came crashing down. Within one year, Groupon lost nearly 85 percent of its market value, plunging from a high of $13 billion to less than $3 billion.[2] The co-founder and CEO Andrew Mason—who hired and took a chance on me—was fired and replaced.[3]

It was time for me to leave Groupon too. After years of working inside other startups, I realized what I really wanted, but had been afraid to do, was to start my own. I now had the experience and what I believed was a winning idea. But I was struggling to get other people excited about the vision. Meanwhile, every day I'd read about new founders receiving funding and wonder, "Why not me?" Even in Silicon Valley—the land of ideas—I was starting to feel the same frustration I had felt sitting in a cubicle in Detroit. I was waiting for someone to pay attention—waiting to be discovered.

More than a year later, standing stage left at FailCon, I

felt my phone vibrate. It was my brother, Sanjay. He's an Emmy Award–winning television reporter, a *New York Times* bestselling author, *and* a neurosurgeon to boot. I'm still trying to make my dad proud, while he's done enough to make an entire subcontinent of fathers proud. "Call you back," I texted. I, too, was very busy. I was about to keynote a conference on failure.

I got through my speech as quickly as possible. Scanning the crowd opportunistically for investors, I somehow missed the reporter scribbling notes. More than a year passed, and I had completely forgotten about FailCon. By that point, I had recruited a small team to work with me on Rise, but the idea still hadn't gained traction. We were struggling to find customers and rapidly running out of money. My co-founder and I needed to raise funding so that we could expand our team, release a great product, and build fruitful partnerships. And if we didn't find that money soon, my startup dream was over.

Then something happened that changed everything. It was a Saturday morning, and I overheard my wife, Leena, on the phone with her mother. "No, we're not moving home, Mom," she said. "Yes, I know San Francisco is very expensive." When I walked into the room, Leena was holding that day's *New York Times* open to a full-length story on failure, with my face at the top.

I had seen mug shots that were more flattering.

The piece went viral. If you googled "failure" at the time, one of your top results would be a full-length *Times* article featuring me. I had spent an entire career trying to craft an image of success. Now I was the poster child for defeat. My inbox was jammed with consolation messages. My parents offered to help pay that month's rent. Old law school professors reached out to help me find a real job. Friends I hadn't spoken to in years simply messaged, "Are you okay?"

Realizing I could no longer hide behind a fake-it-till-you-make-it attitude of success, I decided to give this new identity a try. I began emailing highly successful people using the *Times* article to break the ice. I'd write things like, "As you can see from the article below, I don't know what I'm doing. Would you be willing to grab coffee and give me some advice?"

It worked. That article paved the way to hundreds of open, honest conversations with fascinating people. Founders of unicorn-status startups; producers of Oscar-winning films; culinary icons; members of Congress; executives at iconic companies like Lego and Pixar; even military leaders at the Pentagon.

In the end, I was left with a life-altering discovery. *People who change the world around them aren't just brilliant...they're backable.* They have a seemingly mysterious superpower that lies at the intersection of "creativity" and "persuasion." When backable people express themselves, we feel moved. When they share an idea, we take action.

You probably know someone who seems to be naturally backable. For the record, I am *not* one of those people. I'm an introvert by nature, I look comically young for my age, and I'm prone to caving under pressure—like the time I tanked an interview with Jack Dorsey.

I was interviewing for a product development role with the Twitter founder's newest company, Square. By the time we sat down together, I had spent years leading product teams. Yet I couldn't give a coherent answer to any of his questions—not even the softballs. I was anxious, sweaty, and tongue-tied. During our thirty minutes together, I watched Dorsey's smile fade to neutral and eventually sink into straight confusion.

I was qualified for the role, but I didn't get the job.

We've all had our fair share of Dorsey moments—when something sounded exciting inside your head but uninspiring when it left your mouth. It can feel a lot like trying to insert a crumpled dollar into a vending machine.

But your dollar is worth the same as a crisp, clean bill. We are all within striking range of becoming backable. We just need to make some adjustments to our style, without losing our edge—without sacrificing what makes us who we are.

Inside this book are those adjustments—seven surprising changes that course-corrected my life and career. By taking these steps, I went from feeling embarrassed to speak inside team meetings to confidently pitching ideas inside the offices of people like Michelle Obama and Tim Cook. I went from being the face of failure for the *New York Times* to being named the New Face of Innovation by the New York Stock Exchange magazine.

I went from being rejected by every investor I pitched to raising millions of dollars. The *Today* show featured Rise, and Apple named us the Best New App of the Year. The Obama White House chose us to be its partner for tackling obesity. And ultimately, One Medical, a thriving company en route to an IPO, acquired Rise for multiple times its original value.

Once I realized the power of these adjustments, I couldn't keep them to myself. I had to share it with the world. And not just entrepreneurs, but people from all walks of life—from physicians to musicians, educators to fashion designers. The artist who wants to be featured by her favorite gallery, the accountant who needs a client to act on his recommendation, the nurse who has a new method for lowering her patients' risk of addiction to pain medications. Today I teach the seven steps to becoming backable in hospitals, companies, charities, and studios. I joined the faculty at Harvard University to teach students how to launch backable careers.

Because I'm convinced we all have a brilliant idea tucked away somewhere. Yet most of us are afraid to share it and have it be dismissed. We all know how it feels to be unseen or ignored. To feel like we don't have what it takes.

Untapped genius is not just inside you; it's everywhere. And it comes at a huge cost—to our well-being, to our society, and even to human life.

The morning the space shuttle *Challenger* was launched, NASA engineer Bob Ebeling pounded his car's steering wheel and, with tears in his eyes, said, "Everyone's going to die."[4] The day before, Ebeling had sounded the alarm that the cold temperature expected overnight would stiffen the rubber O-ring seals, causing them to malfunction. He assembled the data, called a meeting, and attempted to persuade his colleagues to delay the launch. It didn't work.

Seventy-three seconds after takeoff, the shuttle disintegrated, killing all seven crew members, including Christa McAuliffe, who would have been the first teacher to travel to space.[5] Ebeling spent the rest of his life blaming himself for his inability to convince the people in that room. Before his death he told NPR, "I think that's one of the mistakes God made. He shouldn't have picked me for that job."[6]

Compare Ebeling for a moment to Billy McFarland, who convinced celebrities, governments, and investors to dump millions of dollars into an idea called the Fyre Festival. McFarland's pitch promised the world's hottest musicians, white-sand beaches, and five-star accommodations. Instead, when guests arrived, they were directed to a disaster relief tent, given a cheese sandwich, and struggled to find clean drinking water. Today, McFarland is serving a six-year prison sentence for fraud—and people are still scratching their heads wondering how an unknown founder with an unsuccessful track record convinced reputable people to give him $26 million in funding.[7]

The world would be a better place if we could transport Billy McFarland's persuasiveness into people like Bob Ebeling. That's why I wrote this book. We need more high-integrity people who know how to sell a good idea.

Damyanti Hingorani, a woman whom *Time* magazine called a "groundbreaker," is one of my favorite backable stories.[8] Hingorani spent her early childhood as a refugee near the border between Pakistan and India. She lived in a home without running water or electricity yet still managed to teach herself how to read. And the first book she read from cover to cover was the biography of Henry Ford. That book inspired a dream, some would say an impossible one, for a young girl in that particular place and time. Hingorani wanted to become an engineer building cars for Ford Motor Company.

She was fortunate to have parents who believed in her. And they saved every penny they had to get her on a boat to America. Years later, on the day she graduated from Oklahoma State University, she boarded a train to Detroit, ready to apply for her dream job.

But this was the 1960s, and while Ford Motor Company was still in its heyday, employing thousands of engineers, not a single one of them was a woman. So when Hingorani finally found herself in a room with a hiring manager, he told her in a polite midwestern kind of way, "I'm sorry...we don't have any female engineers working here."[9]

Deflated, Hingorani picked up her slightly crumpled résumé,

grabbed her purse, and got up to leave the room. But then something clicked. It was as if she suddenly remembered everything it had taken to make it this far. All the sacrifices she had made, that her parents had made. She turned around, looked the hiring manager directly in his eyes, and told him her story. Reading about the Model T late at night near a kerosene lamp...waving goodbye to her parents one last time as she boarded her ship, not knowing if she'd ever see them again...bicycling off campus to use the restroom because her engineering college didn't have one for women. All of it was to be here, in this very room.

Then she said, "If you don't have any female engineers, then do yourself a favor and hire me *now*." It was in that meeting, inside a plain-looking office, that a middle-aged manager from suburban Michigan decided to take a chance on a twenty-four-year-old refugee from the India-Pakistan border. And that's how on August 7, 1967, Damyanti Hingorani became Ford Motor Company's first female engineer.[10]

In the years that followed, Hingorani became a guiding light for immigrants who, too, wanted to believe in a better day. She helped reshape an industry's hiring practices and mentored women of color inside Ford. When she retired, after thirty-five years with the company, she became an inspiring force for Girls Who Code, an organization that has provided technology training to more than three hundred thousand girls around the world.[11]

Hingorani changed everything—for the workforce, for immigrants, for women. She also changed things for me. If Damyanti Hingorani hadn't inspired the hiring manager in that room, if she hadn't made herself backable, I wouldn't be here to write this book. And that is because Damyanti Hingorani is my mom.

When I struggled to be seen, when I was literally a top search result for failure, it was Mom who pushed me to keep going. And it was Mom who made me understand that the opposite of success isn't failure—it's boredom. That you can't wait to be asked to share your ideas, because that day may never come. That in order to succeed, you need to get out and inspire people to see in you what you see in yourself.

This book will show you how.

STEP 1:

CONVINCE YOURSELF FIRST

It was 1969 and President Richard M. Nixon was slashing budgets to pay for the Vietnam War. The Public Broadcasting Service was at the top of his list. PBS had been brought to life by Lyndon Johnson's Great Society, but Nixon viewed it as artsy and unnecessary. His cut required approval from the Senate, which seemed all but a formality because the chair of the Senate Subcommittee on Communications, Senator John Pastore, was a proponent of the war.

The only thing standing in the way was a mild-mannered man who was on a television show that Senator Pastore had never heard of.[1] As the TV host quietly waited to give his testimony, Pastore found it hard to hide his aggression. "All right, Rogers," he said grumpily. "You have the floor."

"Rogers" was none other than Fred Rogers of *Mister Rogers' Neighborhood*. You might know what happened next. Rogers secured PBS's future with a seven-minute speech that has been the subject of articles, books, and viral videos. He is described as "captivating" and "compelling." Iconic shows like *Sesame Street* and *Cosmos* may not have ever come to be had it not been for that single speech.

And yet, if you go back and *watch* Rogers's speech, you might get a different impression. He nervously shifts in his seat and fumbles with his papers. He speaks with a flat, monotone voice and doesn't make use of hand gestures. In many ways, his mannerisms are the opposite of what you'd learn from public speaking courses like Toastmasters or Dale Carnegie. So what was it about this speech that made it so influential?

When I began writing this book, I assumed I'd find a certain *style* to how backable people communicate their ideas—a way of utilizing eye contact, hand gestures, and pacing—to charm their audience. However, after digging deeper, I came to realize that this is not the case at all.

Watch the number one TED Talk of all time[2] and you might be surprised to see Sir Ken Robinson stand with a slight slouch and a hand in his pocket while he explores whether schools kill creativity. View Elon Musk unveiling the future of SpaceX and you might agree with *Inc.* magazine's headline that he "Fails Public Speaking 101."[3] Search the transcript of the original iPhone launch and you might be surprised to find that Steve Jobs said "uh" at least eighty times.[4]

Yet Robinson has held the top TED spot for years, Musk's forty-minute presentation has about 2 million views,[5] and Jobs's iPhone launch is one of most widely discussed product announcements of all time.

What moves people isn't charisma, but conviction. Backable people earnestly believe in what they're saying, and they simply let that belief shine through whatever style feels most natural. If you don't truly believe in what you're saying, there is no slide fancy enough, no hand gesture compelling enough, to save you. If you want to convince others, you must convince yourself first.

Preparing my pitch for Rise, I spent a lot of time focusing on the bells and whistles of the presentation. I pulled together an impressive-looking slide deck with beautiful visuals. I came up with attention-grabbing taglines. I practiced hand gestures in front of a mirror.

But pitches aren't monologues. They're a back-and-forth, typically with people who know how to ask tough questions. And while my initial fifteen-minute presentation typically went fine, things tended to unravel in the next forty-five minutes of Q&A.

Now I understand why. Peter Chernin is a legendary media executive who has produced Oscar-nominated films like *Hidden Figures, The Greatest Showman,* and *Ford v Ferrari,* while also investing in startups like Pandora, Headspace, and Barstool Sports. Chernin told me that when he's undecided on whether to back an idea, he'll sometimes look at the film-maker or entrepreneur and say, "That's the stupidest idea I've ever heard." Then he'll wait to see if they back down or show conviction.

Had that happened to me when I was first pitching Rise, I would have dropped into the fetal position. I may have had fancy slides, but I didn't have high conviction. I was trying to convince others without convincing myself first. When I realized how important that was to being backable, I set out to learn how backable people build conviction in a new idea.

SCHEDULE INCUBATION TIME

On February 15, 2010, in the Basque countryside of northern Spain, a two-star Michelin restaurant named Mugaritz burned to the ground. It took firefighters two hours and five sets of equipment to put out the flames, but it was too late.

The essential parts of Mugaritz's restaurant—including its kitchen—were destroyed and would take several months to rebuild. But despite having no source of income during this costly restoration, the owner, Chef Andoni Aduriz, continued to pay his 40 employees.[6] Aduriz was beloved by chefs around the world, and when word got out that Mugaritz was on the verge of closing permanently, restaurants from Japan to Venezuela stepped in to help him cover reconstruction expenses. Still, Aduriz knew that once Mugaritz reopened, the restaurant would need to thrive in order to make up for all that was lost.

The chef pulled together his team and announced that not a moment over the following four months would go to waste. They didn't have a restaurant, customers, or even a full kitchen—the only thing that they had left was their ideas. They would use this time to go back to the drawing board. To reflect on what they had learned and bring forth concepts that had previously seemed impossible.

Four months later, when Mugaritz reopened its doors, Aduriz and his team had reinvented the restaurant—from the way they set the table to the very core of their culinary experience. Prior to the fire, you'd receive two menus—one with more classical cuisine, the other with more adventurous dishes. After the fire, Mugaritz ditched the safe menu so that when you walked into the restaurant, it was all adventure. Why? Because during those months the team assembled so many creative, unique offerings that they no longer had a desire to play it safe.

A decade later, Aduriz told me how those months were an inflection point for the restaurant and for his culinary philosophy. "Destruction and creation go hand in hand," he said. "The fire actually made us rebuild ourselves by being more faithful to ourselves, to what we really wanted to be."

That's why as the one-year anniversary of the fire approached, Aduriz did something that confused foodies and frustrated a few unknowing tourists. He *voluntarily* closed Mugaritz again for several months to reinvent their menu, just as they had after the fire. Since then, Mugaritz has shut its doors for three months every single year. And for each of those years, Mugaritz has been named one of the top ten restaurants in the world—the only one to stay on the list for 14 years.[7]

Backable people tend to behave a lot like Chef Aduriz. They're constantly tracking ideas on their phone or notepad and then taking them into an incubation period. Instead of rushing out to share them immediately, they nurture and build their ideas behind the scenes. Bill Gates, whom we'll discuss again later, takes "think weeks," where he goes off the grid with a pile of books and a goal to open himself up to new ideas.[8] Paul Graham, one of the founders of Y Combinator, a startup accelerator that's spawned companies like Instacart, Stripe, DoorDash, and Dropbox, says that instead of rushing out to investors, founders would be much better off if they took the quiet time to understand *why* their startup is worth investing in.[9]

When an idea first enters your mind, it's not fully formed, and certainly not prepared to interact with the real world. But because we're excited about the possibility, we make the mistake of inviting people in when the idea isn't ready. Every time I'm fired up about a new idea, I feel an impulse to share it immediately.

But at this premature stage, even the most positive-intentioned reaction can crush the spirit of an idea. If you don't get the reaction you're looking for, it can instantly deflate your energy. Moreover, you haven't taken the time to articulate what's inside your head, so you share it in a half-baked way—expecting a fully baked response. When that reaction doesn't come, it saps your enthusiasm.

Imagine you wake up one morning, grab a cup of coffee, and out of nowhere an idea hits you. Your eyes brighten. You jump in your car and head to the office, where you bump into your manager, Tricia. You can't help telling her that you came up with "the most interesting idea." She doesn't interrupt, so you begin to share your brand-new way for people on the team to give one another feedback. It would be anonymous, super simple to use, all through text messaging. Best of all, you won't have to wait for performance reviews to figure out what your team thinks of you. At this point, your voice is inflecting, and you're smiling at the genius of your idea.

Then it happens. Tricia asks, "How would this system know *when* to gather feedback from your colleague?" You think for a moment. "That's an interesting question," you say. "Well, I guess it would happen every few months. Or maybe we could automatically trigger a notification based on...You know what, I've got to think about that some more." Tricia stares at you blankly, then gives you a deadpan "Hm."

Years of coaching people inside companies has made me realize something: most new ideas aren't killed inside conference rooms. They're killed inside hallways and break rooms. They're shared before they really had a chance to mature. And when we don't get the reaction we want, we tend to put our concepts inside a drawer. But it's not that our idea was bad—it simply wasn't ready to share.

Incubation time isn't critical just for entrepreneurs. Around 2017, for the first time in a decade, LEGO was seeing a drop in sales and profits.[10] Rémi Marcelli, a self-educated advertising exec who had been hired a year before to head up the Danish toy maker's in-house marketing and communication agency, was asked by the company's leadership to help find an answer.[11] But instead of offering a clear picture for the path ahead, he completely shook things up at the eighty-year-old company.

"I don't jump to conclusions, I jump to experimentation," Marcelli told me. That's why, amid a slowdown, Marcelli proposed that the company also slow down. He advocated for a full two-month pause on all operations in his division so that he and his team could take incubation time and come back with an idea.

With hesitant approval from management, Marcelli approached his pause a lot like Chef Aduriz. At Mugaritz, the culinary team would begin their incubation period with around one hundred ideas and end it feeling convinced by around fifty. These tend to be the dishes that Aduriz considers the most thought-provoking—the ones that will fully tap each of your senses. In one of their incubation periods, Aduriz and team deliberately exposed fresh fruit to edible fungus. Later, Instagram was ablaze with photos of rotten fruit that tasted like dessert, called "Noble Rot."[12]

Just like Aduriz, Marcelli and his LEGO team trimmed a laundry list of ideas down to a handful, including one that was sure to rattle some people inside the company. For nearly the company's entire history, the various LEGO lines, each in its own geography, would create their own siloed marketing campaigns, targeted to their very specific customer market. But during their incubation time, Marcelli and the team built conviction behind the idea to run bigger, top-level promotional campaigns created around passion points. Even though these campaigns wouldn't be customized for each line or gender or age, they would be less formulaic and, they believed, would generate more buzz. By the end of the pause, Marcelli had run enough experiments and built enough conviction that this was the best way to showcase new ideas coming out of the LEGO brand.

Marcelli was about to propose breaking a formula that had worked for years. Had he shared this idea before taking incubation time, it almost certainly would have been shot down. Had he even *hinted* at the idea up front, he might have been told not to waste time pursuing it. But by not blurting out his idea, and instead giving it the time and space it needed to be tested and improved, Marcelli and his team entered the room confident in their conclusions. They broke a multidecade tradition inside a dominant industry player by convincing themselves first.

With a new way of working, LEGO reversed its revenues and profits from declining in 2017 to a period of growth in 2018 and 2019, even as the toy landscape had become more challenging with retailers like Toys"R"Us closing.[13] And if you visit LEGO's headquarters today, you'll see mini incubation periods happening across the company from the innovation team to the IT department.

I wish I had taken more incubation time for Rise. After coming up with the idea, I was so excited that I couldn't wait to share it with others. Within a couple of weeks I was reaching out to potential investors, asking them to meet for coffee. If you were to look back on the year when I struggled to raise money, you'd find that I spent more than 80 percent of my time on the investor pitch deck, and the remaining time incubating the actual concept. I spent almost all my time working to convince investors and very little time working to convince myself.

Reverse that. Spend at least 80 percent of your time convincing yourself, then the remainder pulling together the slides, business plans, or whatever else you need to convince a backer. You're much better off walking into a room with high conviction and low-production-value material than the other way around.

One thing to note about both Chef Aduriz and Rémi Marcelli is that their incubation time had an end date...it wasn't endless. Chef Aduriz set a fixed date to reopen Mugaritz, and Marcelli had a scheduled time to present his strategy to LEGO's top brass. Without establishing a deadline for your incubation time, it's easy to sit on an idea without ever pushing it forward. As a matter of discipline, backable people avoid an "as long as it takes" approach and mark a deadline on their calendars. By then, either you have conviction for your idea, or it's time to move on.

I've seen this work across industries. Troy Carter, a record producer and investor who's worked with stars like Tupac Shakur and Will Smith, says he backed Lady Gaga because she had a sense of urgency and focus.[14] It turns out that was because Gaga was on a fixed timeline. She had just been dropped by Def Jam Records and was sleeping on her grandmother's couch. Gaga's father saw his daughter struggling and gave her one year to land another recording contract—or she'd have to go back to school.[15] It worked. Not only is Lady Gaga one of the world's all-time bestselling artists; she's also one of *Time* magazine's Top 10 College Dropouts.[16]

STEER INTO OBJECTIONS

While working at Mozilla, I built a startup on the side called the Kahani Movement. We made documentary films easier to create with open-source software. It was a fun idea that got admitted to South by Southwest (SXSW), but I never figured out a way to monetize it. It did, however, put me on the radar of Reid Hoffman, co-founder of LinkedIn, who was also passionate about new ways to open-source creativity. My idea died, but Hoffman became a friend and mentor.

When Rise was being rejected by investors, Hoffman shared one of the keys to his success in the pitch room. "There will be one to three issues that are potentially problematic for your financing," Hoffman said to me. "Address them head on."

Hoffman had first put this into practice as a junior-level employee inside Apple. "I wanted to be a product manager, but I didn't have the right background," he told me. That was a problem because the hiring team was inundated with qualified candidates. Hoffman knew that trying to outcompete the others based on his résumé wasn't going to work. So when he approached James Isaacs, Apple's eWorld group's head of product management, Hoffman told me that he decided to try something new—he steered straight into the obvious objection. "Look, I know I don't have any product management experience," he said. "So, what if I pulled together a detailed document outlining my ideas? If I did that, would you take a look?"

Isaacs agreed, and a few days later, Hoffman returned with his ideas. The document clearly wasn't written by someone with highly relevant experience, but it showed Isaacs that Hoffman had real potential. That was the start of Hoffman's career in product management. By addressing his lack of experience head on, rather than trying to hide it, he turned a potential skeptic into one of his earliest professional backers—someone who helped lay the foundation for his career.

Years later, when Hoffman co-founded LinkedIn, he knew investors' biggest concern would be revenue. "They were still licking their wounds from the dot-com bust," he said. Investors were now focused on "proven business models" and "we didn't have a dime of revenue."

But instead of veering away from the revenue question, he hit it directly. He began his pitch by acknowledging the lack of revenue and then quickly showcased three potential ways LinkedIn could make money—from ads, listings, and subscriptions. By addressing the objection before the investors could even bring it up, Hoffman earned enough trust that he would be able to figure it out.

One final note from Hoffman (for now) is to hit the objections sooner rather than later. "You have the most attention from investors in the first few minutes," he says. "Most investors arrive with questions, and if you proactively show you understand their principal concerns, you earn their attention for the rest of the pitch."

Though I typically use slides to pitch a new idea, I don't think they're very useful for helping me prepare. Slides let you steer away from the objections because you can hide behind high-level bullets and fancy visuals. This is one of the reasons Jeff Bezos did away with slides during his senior team meetings.[17]

As Amazon grew beyond books, Bezos was constantly being pitched new ideas by employees—for new product lines, income streams, and technology capabilities. But Bezos, who's known to be hypercritical inside the pitch room, felt that people were unprepared to answer his questions.

So he shifted Amazon's pitch process from slides to a written narrative. If you had a new concept to share with Bezos, you needed to explain it in a thoughtful three- to five-page document using full sentences and paragraphs. "If someone builds a list of bullet points in Word, that would be just as bad as PowerPoint," said Bezos when he announced the change.[18]

Senior executives who were there for the shift from slides to narratives told me that while the quality of the ideas didn't change, the quality of the explanations became significantly stronger. One former Amazon executive told me, "After writing a narrative, I always felt better prepared to answer Jeff's questions."

While bullets share *what* you believe, fully formed paragraphs force you to explain *why*. When I write a new narrative, I force myself to come up with at least three key objections to my idea and then answer them in fully formed sentences. Now that I can't use bullets, I'm forced to use words like "because" and actually explain my thinking. I rarely share my narratives with anyone else. They are simply my personal tool to convince myself first.

When I began pitching Rise, I did my best to avoid the objections, hoping investors wouldn't bring them up. They always did, and when I couldn't answer them, they became "gotcha" moments that completely sank my idea.

After hearing Hoffman's story, I took a pause in my fundraising process to think about the critics and steer directly into the objections. Rise matched customers with personal nutritionists, and while I had a solid plan for recruiting nutritionists, I didn't know how we were going to find customers. Advertising in the weight-loss space is expensive and inundated with competition from big brands like Weight Watchers (WW) and Jenny Craig.

So I set aside two weeks of incubation time to come up with scrappier ways to reach customers. Like Chef Aduriz, I wanted to test a list of ideas quickly. One initial thought was to have doctors refer patients to us. But after surveying more than a dozen doctors, I discovered that they were already being bombarded for referrals by lots of healthcare startups.

I moved on to testing other avenues and eventually found one with real potential. One of my friends had just run a race called the Tough Mudder. He showed me photos of thousands of people gathered at the starting line of one of their races outside Chicago. I did some research and realized that marathons, triathlons, and races like the Tough Mudder were growing at a breakneck pace. What if we matched people who were training with their own personal nutritionists? I began cold-calling organizers of races and received positive responses. I ran a lightweight Facebook ad focused on racers and found that people were clicking through.

When I went back out to investors, I no longer avoided the customer-acquisition question; I steered straight into it. I first acknowledged that this was still an unsolved problem but then showed the trend line of races like the Tough Mudder and the results of the tests we'd run. It was by no means a perfect answer to the objection. But by steering into it rather than avoiding it, I gained credibility and settled some questions that would have otherwise nagged at potential investors. Instead, I captured their attention for the stronger points of my pitch.

THROWAWAY WORK

Salman Rushdie is a bestselling author, has won the Booker Prize, and was knighted by the queen of England for his services to literature. He's also a personal favorite. When I was in law school in Chicago, I discovered that Rushdie was passing through town. I frantically scoured the web for his email address and pleaded with him to meet me for coffee. He kindly relented and gave me fifteen minutes between meetings. I could tell he regretted his decision when the first question I asked was, "How do you get inspired to write?"

He took a moment to make direct eye contact so that I would remember what he was about to say. "I don't get inspired to write. I just write." Rushdie went on to tell me that he sits down at his desk every morning, just like anyone else. Most of what he produces isn't usable, but buried in each day's pile is a small pearl he's convinced is worth keeping. Over the years, he's strung those pearls together to create pages, chapters, and more than a dozen novels.

Working through a new idea is an active process—it's not simply batting things around in your head. It's actually starting your project—through writing, drawing, lines of code, or whatever—so that you have enough to take a step back and ask, "Am I headed in the right direction?" One of the reasons this is hard for people, including me, is because the answer might be "No," and then we'll feel like we've wasted our time.

When I was six years old, I visited my family in New Delhi. They had just bought their very first television set—a black-and-white TV with a "bunny-ears" antenna wired up to the roof of the home. The connection was always a bit fuzzy, so my cousins and I would race to the roof together, adjust the bunny ears, and then race back down the stairs to observe the result. But sometimes adjusting the bunny ears wasn't enough. No matter how we tweaked them, there was still some fuzz on the TV. On those occasions, we needed to move the antenna to a completely different spot on the roof and start the adjustments from scratch.

Most of us are afraid to put things down on paper because we might see the result and realize we can't just play around with the bunny ears; we have to move the antenna and start over. But a big part of convincing yourself is accepting that throwaway work is a natural part of the process. By the time I handed this book in to my editor, I had cut more than one hundred pages of material. But it took me seeing these paragraphs on the page to know they didn't work. Adjusting them wasn't going to remove the fuzziness—I had to scrap them and start over.

If the idea of throwaway work is as off-putting to you as it initially was to me, then maybe Shawn Ryan's story will help. As a struggling television writer, Ryan wrote sixteen teleplays on spec and not only did none of them make it on the air, they didn't earn him a dime. But by the time he wrote his last two—one for *NYPD Blue*, the other for *The Larry Sanders Show*—Ryan says he finally found his voice. Those scripts caught the attention of the creators of *Nash Bridges*, a crime drama starring Don Johnson. They gave Ryan his first staff job as a professional writer.

During his free time Ryan kept writing and incubating new ideas. He began to build conviction for a new idea about a rogue cop named Vic Mackey who leads the LAPD's strike team and is also being investigated for corruption. FX bought the show, and Ryan became creator and showrunner for *The Shield*. It received six Emmy nominations and became one of the first television shows to lure movie stars, like Glenn Close and Forest Whitaker, to the small screen.

Ryan became known around Hollywood as an overnight success, but the truth is it took him years of throwaway work. When I asked Ryan about all the other scripts, he told me that "none of that effort was wasted" because it all led him to *The Shield*.

His advice to up-and-coming writers (or anyone with an idea): "Do the work before you share with the outside world. You need to be the most passionate advocate. You need to be inspired before you inspire anyone else." In other words, be willing to do the work necessary to convince yourself first.

MEASURE YOUR EMOTIONAL RUNWAY

In the startup world, one of the things we obsess about is "financial runway"—having enough money in the bank to keep making progress and payroll. But what we don't talk about enough is "emotional runway." This is the energy we have left to keep pushing a new idea forward.

Over the years, I've seen more founders run out of energy than run out of money. Bringing a new idea into the world requires a tremendous amount of stamina. You're on the receiving end of doubts, conflicts, and deadlines—and yet you're still required to maintain a high level of conviction and confidence. The only way your energy stays high is if it's replenished by your own passion for the idea. Intellectual interest is important, but it's rarely enough—you need to be emotionally invested.

Psychologists have long argued that our brain is made up of two systems—a rational system and an emotional system. In his book *The Happiness Hypothesis,* social psychologist

Jonathan Haidt describes these systems as a rider on top of an elephant. Your rider represents your rational side that likes to analyze problems, weigh options, and argue solutions. But it's your elephant, your more emotional side, that gives you the energy to keep running with a new idea.[19]

In the early days of a new concept, we may be completely in tune with our elephant. We get excited about a vision, a possibility. But as we dig deeper into practicalities like the business model and operations, our rider takes over. We become fixated on the logic of an idea and often lose sight of the emotion.

But convincing yourself requires both. It's not enough to figure out whether your idea fits the market—you have to figure out whether an idea fits *you*. Does it stoke something deep inside you? Lin-Manuel Miranda says he "falls in love for a living." Ideas like *Hamilton* take years to create, so Miranda says when you have an idea, "you really have to fall in love with it."[20]

And backers can tell when you're in love with your idea. That's why investors are often attracted to founders with a personal attachment to their business. Margit Wennmachers, an operating partner at venture capital firm Andreessen Horowitz, recently told me about Propel, a startup that helps low-income Americans manage their food stamps. When the founder, Jimmy Chen, pitched the partners on the idea, it was clear his emotional ties to the subject ran deep, partly because when he was growing up, his family sometimes struggled to put food on the table.[21]

You don't need personal history in order to feel personal passion. But your idea needs to strike an emotional chord. Davis Guggenheim, the Oscar-winning director of *An Inconvenient Truth* and *Inside Bill's Brain,* told me "we all have different voices in our head." He says his "clever voice" is always saying things like "that's a cool shot" or "no one's ever done that before." But Guggenheim says he does his best to tune out his clever voice and tune in to how an idea makes him feel. "If something keeps me up at night. If something makes me angry or makes me cry . . . those raw instinctual attachments have never let me down."

So, as you're figuring out whether an idea fits you, ask yourself if you've fallen in love with it. And as you dig in deeper, keep checking in with your elephant, paying attention to whether new challenges are fueling you or depleting you.

I can tell you I have been guilty of letting my rational rider completely take over. When I was considering a new startup, I created a spreadsheet of business ideas. The columns were all the classic entrepreneurship factors—things like market size (the bigger the better) and competition (the smaller the better).

But when I shared this spreadsheet with a mentor, she asked me a simple question: "Which one of these ideas lights you on fire?" After scanning the spreadsheet, a harsh reality hit me: none of them did. At the time I was working at Groupon, and all the ideas in my mind were related to e-commerce. But while I was intellectually interested in e-commerce, I wasn't in love with the market.

Had I pursued one of those ideas, I would have quickly run out of emotional runway. I scrapped my spreadsheet and created a new one. This one didn't include factors like market size and competition. Column A listed "Ideas" and Column B answered a simple question: In love? (yes or no). That exercise forced me to begin reflecting on ideas that truly made me come alive. And then I remembered how a nutritionist helped save my father's life.

STEP 2:

CAST A CENTRAL CHARACTER

In the startup world, Kirsten Green is known as a kingmaker. She launched Forerunner Ventures in 2010 and has since invested in more than eighty companies and led efforts to raise more than $650 million. She has been named one of *Time* magazine's 100 Most Influential People, and VC (Venture Capitalist) of the Year by TechCrunch.

Early in her career, Green was told about a new razor-blade startup but decided she had "zero interest" in investing. Green's background as an analyst informed her thinking: razor blades were a low-margin offering and not a clear fit for e-commerce. Besides, even if the startup got off the ground, they'd have to compete head-to-head with marketing giants like Gillette.

But just two days after hearing about the razor-blades concept, she wound up at a dinner party in San Francisco with the company's founder, Michael Dubin. And within ten minutes of hearing Dubin's pitch in person, Green decided she had to write him a check. Green told me she left that chance conversation thinking, "I have to be in business with him."

Dubin didn't change her mind by saying, "We want to disrupt a multibillion-dollar market with a better, cheaper razor blade sold online." Instead, he introduced Green to his central character—a twenty-something male who takes an active interest in his own health—including what he puts in his body, and what he puts *on* his body. He also values convenience and privacy way more than his father or grandfather did. Then, after setting up his central character, Dubin went through his character's frustrating and cumbersome step-by-step experience of buying razor blades inside a pharmacy. He searches outdated shelves looking for the shaving section. When he finally finds the razor blades, he realizes they are behind a locked security case. He pushes a button for help, alerting everyone in the store that he needs to get behind the glass case—which, by the way, doesn't contain just razors, but also condoms and laxatives. He stands idle in the aisle being judged by others, but not able to move because he doesn't want to miss the employee with the key. That employee finally shows up, annoyed to be pulled away from another task, and then literally watches over his shoulder as he makes his purchase decision.

He gave such vivid detail that it became obvious why the entire experience needed to be disrupted. Rather than saying something general like "The experience is inconvenient and outdated," he gave Green a highly visual walk-through, then let her draw that conclusion for herself. And with that, Dubin made razor blades sexy to an investor whose mission it is to "rewrite the rules of culture."[1]

As individuals, we're wired to care about the stories of individuals. This goes back to life around the campfire—it's in our DNA. When a movie makes us emotional, it's typically because we feel connected to a specific character—rather than the ensemble. Or, imagine two news reports. The first is that a plane went down in the Andes carrying fifty passengers, all presumably alive. The second is that a plane went down in the Andes carrying one passenger, who is presumably alive. All of a sudden, we want to know who this one person is, where they're from, and why they were traveling to the Andes in the first place.

This is why a reporter will cover a trend through the eyes of one person. Trish Hall, a former op-ed editor at the *New York Times*, says, "You don't go into journalism without feeling like facts change the world." And yet, Hall says, "facts alone will not change people's minds. Emotions and feelings are just as important, probably more important."[2]

Not long after that dinner, Green became the lead backer in Dollar Shave Club's first investment round and joined Dubin's board. Four years later the company was sold to Unilever for $1 billion.

CHOOSE ONE PERSON

Bill Gates once showed his daughter a video of a young girl with polio. The girl was holding a pair of dilapidated wooden crutches and trying to walk down a dirt road. After watching the video, his daughter turned to her father and said, "Well, what did you do?"[3] Gates told his daughter his foundation was eradicating polio. He shared the numbers with her—the hundreds of millions of dollars they were deploying, the goals they'd set, and the metrics they'd already hit, including shrinking the number of cases in Nigeria from seven hundred per year to fewer than thirty. "No, no, no," interrupted Gates's daughter. She pointed back to the video and asked, "What did you do for *her*?"

Great storytellers don't just focus on a central character, but also a central reader. Instead of addressing millions of people, they'll imagine they're sharing the story with one specific person. Tim Ferriss really helped me understand this.

By the time we met, Ferriss had invested in dozens of startups including Facebook, Shopify, and Twitter. I thought he'd be the perfect backer for Rise, but he didn't quite agree. Another "pass." But during our conversation he shared a story that changed the way I think about pitching an idea. I didn't realize this at the time, but *The 4-Hour Workweek*, which had spent nearly five years as a *New York Times* bestseller, was rejected by 26 publishers in a row.[4]

Ferriss told me that his first attempt to write the book had failed completely. "I was trying to write for as many people as possible," he said. As a result, the storytelling felt flat and impersonal. That's when Ferriss shifted his approach. Instead of writing for a broad audience, he decided to write for two specific friends—one an entrepreneur, the other working at a bank. Both felt trapped in their jobs. Ferriss sat down at his laptop and composed an email to them, which evolved into a chapter in his book.

Writing with a specific person in mind made the storytelling sharper and more compelling. And the punchline was that even though Ferriss wrote the book for two friends, one of the most common pieces of feedback he receives is "I felt like you were writing it just to me."[5]

I learned this lesson just in time to help a first-time startup founder with his pitch. Daniel had just left his engineering role at Uber and was being swarmed with recruiting calls to get him to join another company. But he was waiting on something else—a call back from investors.

Daniel had a new idea—think of it like Fidelity for millennials. The goal was to help people pay down their student loan debt through zero-fee investments. You choose your asset allocation and the service automatically lets you know when it's time to rebalance through the app.

We met near the Embarcadero in San Francisco at a coffee shop known for pitch meetings. I arrived early and just listened to the symphony of pitches happening all around me. Every table was something different, but "block chain" was the loudest instrument. Deep in thought, I was startled when Daniel tapped me on the shoulder. He was energetic and smiley, showing none of the frustration I'd picked up on the phone.

But five minutes into his practice pitch I was already lost. He was clearly excited about an idea. But I couldn't really understand what the idea was. He was throwing big numbers my way and getting into the details of his product, when I asked him if we could take a pause. He agreed, and I asked him whom he was building this service for. His answer was one that I would hear many times again: "Millennials."

"Pick one of those millennials." I said. "Someone you know really well who's going to use your product. Someone whose life is going to change because of your idea."

After a moment, Daniel chose his ex-girlfriend Katie.

"Great. Tell me about Katie."

"Well. Okay..." I could hear the confusion in his voice. How was any of this going to help him make a *business* case for his idea? I asked him to trust me. After all, I had no interest other than to see his pitch succeed.

After a slow sip of overpriced flavored green tea, Daniel

began to tell me about Katie. Her father was an electrician, her mom was a teacher. "A real salt-of-the-earth family," he said. Then it came—the core of why Daniel was starting this company. "When Katie was fifteen, her father started to experience severe joint pain. It got so bad that he could no longer carry heavy equipment, climb ladders, or squat down underneath a machine. Their income dropped, while their hospital bills rose." As Daniel went deeper into Katie's story, his demeanor changed. He was more sincere and passionate—and the reason why he was starting this business became apparent.

When Daniel met Katie in college, she was working a full-time job to avoid student loans because she had seen what debt did to her family. Still, she graduated with more than $40,000 of loan debt. Over the next ten years, living paycheck to paycheck, Katie served as a social worker helping people deal with their own financial problems. During that time, what she owed to creditors nearly doubled.

Good stories help you see the character in the story. Great stories help you see yourself in the story. As Daniel spoke, I flashed back to my wife and me at an ATM machine in the River North area of Chicago. It was snowing outside, and we were trying to grab some cash quickly and go. We had begun to talk about starting a family, and money was on my mind. When I checked my account balance, it was less than $3,000—and we owed at least $30,000 in student loans. Anxiety would be an unfair simplification of what I experienced at that moment. I felt every word of Katie's story.

Then Daniel hit me with the numbers. "In the United States, over 50 million people are living Katie's life." If his first pitch was the Ugly Duchess, this was the Mona Lisa.

CREATE A STORYBOARD

Startup ideas tend to come in waves. Better mattresses. Smarter toothbrushes. Kid-friendly social networks. A couple of years ago, "suitcase startups" seemed to be the thing.

One investor told me that her firm received multiple suitcase startup pitches in a period of four months. The team was somewhat interested in the suitcase space—they were high-margin goods that felt logical to sell online. The problem was that all of these pitch decks seemed to say almost exactly the same thing, something along the lines of: "We want to disrupt a massive multibillion-dollar market."

But one pitch stood out from the pack. This pitch made the customer, not the market, the star. As Michael Dubin did for Dollar Shave Club, this pitch visually walked through a sample customer's story—what she ate for brunch (avocado toast), what kind of dog she had (cute, but rescued), and the next dream destination on her list (Iceland). Jen Rubio, the startup's co-founder, even created an Instagram account, packed with posts, to tell her customer's story.

"The whole idea was much bigger; it wasn't about a suitcase," the investor told me. Her firm wrote the first institutional check to Away, which became the hottest luggage company in the market.

While the Away pitch was different enough to stand out, it followed a clear pattern among highly backable people. They don't just give a quick description of their customer; they visually walk you through the customer's experience. I've come to call this technique storyboarding and have seen that it's convincing not just to investors, but to recruits, partners, and colleagues as well. Michael Dubin told me he didn't stop storyboarding after he raised his first round of funding for Dollar Shave Club. Instead, he continued to cast a central character in all of his marketing and ads, which have been viewed tens of millions of times. Maybe that's also why storyboarding has been such a central part of the Airbnb story. About eight years ago, I visited Airbnb's first major office in Potrero Hill and saw illustrations on the wall that storyboarded *every* major detail for an Airbnb host:

> You talk to friends who've done it before to hear what their experience was like.
>
> You decide to give it a try and upload details and photos for your home.
>
> You receive an inbound inquiry from an interested guest and check out their profile.
>
> You move forward with a transaction and receive a payment.
>
> The big day arrives, and you greet your guest to personally hand them a key.
>
> You return after the two-day stay and inspect your place.
>
> You open the Airbnb app to leave your guest a review and see how they reviewed you.

The inspiration for the Airbnb storyboard came from Disney.[6] During a holiday break, the CEO, Brian Chesky, read a biography of Walt Disney and was especially taken by the comic-book-style outline he used to get his colleagues on the same page for the studio's first feature-length movie, *Snow White*. Inspired by Disney's tool, Chesky hired an animator from Pixar to help him build his first storyboards.[7]

As they had for Disney, storyboards helped the company

identify key moments in the experience that needed extra focus. For the host, it was when they received their payment and quickly made the decision whether to re-list their property. For the guest, it was their first minute walking into the home. By visualizing every step, Airbnb could pinpoint where to reinvent the experience in a way that everyone understood, whether you were a designer, a salesperson, or an engineer.

And that's the thing about storyboards—they serve as an "empathy bridge" between your backer and your customer—just as a short video served as a bridge between Bill Gates's daughter and a girl she didn't know in Nigeria. They help us see what someone else sees and feel what they feel. That's especially important inside a pitch, because most of the time, your backer isn't your customer. Venture capitalists back apps they wouldn't personally use. Publishers back books they might not read. Studio heads back films that they themselves might not watch. In these cases, a storyboard helps put the backer in the shoes of the person you want to serve.

After learning this technique, I stuck a series of Post-it notes across my bedroom wall to visualize the experience of a prototypical Rise customer. The story began with a primary care physician telling my customer that he needs to lose fifteen pounds to lower his risk for diabetes. My customer goes home, searches online for different types of diets, and settles on a modified version of the keto diet. Motivated by some of the stories he's read, he creates a shopping list and goes to Trader Joe's. After powering through the first couple of weeks of the new diet, he feels great. But by week four, at the end of busy days, he's gone back to full-carb plates. By week six, he's given up altogether.

When I later walked rooms of investors through this storyboard, there were nods. They could relate. Storyboarding has a way of creating empathy between your backer and the person you want to serve. Once you've established that empathy, you can talk numbers in a much more powerful way.

Remember: a well-told story isn't a substitute for the facts and figures of your pitch. The elephant and the rider both matter. That's why it was only after the Away team introduced backers to the traveler they imagined that they could share that travel is trending to be a top use of discretionary income for millennials. And it was why once Michael Dubin established Dollar Shave Club's central character, he could share that millions of men in the United States alone go through the in-store razor-blade-buying experience every month. It's also why when a founder named Rahul Vohra pitched a fast-growing email service called Superhuman, he took investors visually into the inbox of a single customer; then he zoomed them out to the fact that across the workforce more than 1 billion people spend three hours of their day reading and writing emails. "That compelled me," serial entrepreneur and partner at First Round Capital Bill Trenchard told me. "It emotionally moved me to make an investment way before there was any evidence that it would work."

Again, the numbers are essential, particularly as an idea matures. But in the early stages of a new idea, it's the customer story that draws people in. Russ Heddleston is the CEO of DocSend, a service that allows you to securely send documents via email. Tens of thousands of investor decks and term sheets have been shared over the service, which gave Heddleston an idea. What if he could figure out which type of pitch decks were finding success and which were falling flat? Heddleston partnered with Harvard Business School and, with permission, analyzed thousands of startup pitch decks to understand how attributes like length, format, and use of imagery affected the likelihood of an investment.[8]

As an analytical guy himself, Heddleston paid particularly close attention to how the decks made use of financials and numbers. But it turned out most successful pitch decks weren't leading with the numbers or the financials. In fact, most pitch decks didn't even include financials. Instead they used a story to hook an investor's interest enough to set up a meeting, where they could then likely share more of the numbers. Those findings surprised Heddleston and most of the startup community. When he published his results in an article on TechCrunch it became one of the site's most heavily shared posts that year.[9]

KEEP YOUR CHARACTER IN SIGHT

A strong central character doesn't just help build a pitch deck. It helps build marketing campaigns, investment approaches, and shareholder relationships—and even serves as a powerful recruiting message.

The job that pulled Leena and me out of student loan debt was my role at Groupon. The year I joined, *Forbes* put the founder, Andrew Mason, on its cover.[10] And yet when I interviewed with Mason, he never even mentioned the company's explosive growth, the massive market size, or the fact that revenue was more than doubling every month.

Instead, Mason told me about the baker whose shop was a few blocks away from the startup's headquarters. "He didn't open a bakery because he loves marketing, or because he loves figuring out how to do customer acquisition," Mason told me. "He opened a bakery because he loves to bake. We exist as a business to take care of all of the other stuff so that he can focus on what he loves."

During the interview, instead of sitting down at a desk or inside a conference room, we walked around downtown Chicago, and Mason told me about the owners of local restaurants, shops, and exercise studios that used Groupon. When we went back to the office, I noticed that the walls weren't decorated with motivational posters. Instead, they were filled with stories of local owners, mom-and-pop shops—reminding every employee every day of the central character they were there to serve.

I had been considering other jobs, but on that day, I decided to move to Chicago and work for Mason. Not because of the numbers or logic, but because of the central character he introduced me to during our interview. I knew that was the person I wanted to help serve.

But over time, it became harder and harder to keep our focus on our central character. As the company grew from one hundred employees to more than ten thousand, and went from small startup to IPO, our primary focus shifted from serving local businesses to serving quarterly performance. It seemed to me that we lost the high level of empathy we had for the struggling mom-and-pop shop and instead squeezed out profit margins at the expense of the very people we were there to serve. As a result, we lost our central character's trust, along with half the company's valuation. With that, I saw company morale sink, investor confidence evaporate, our best people begin to leave, and Mason part ways with the company he founded.

A central character is so powerful that it can build and unravel entire cultures. In 2017 a video emerged of Travis Kalanick, Uber's then CEO, yelling at a well-dressed man.[11] But it wasn't just anyone—it was an Uber driver. Within moments of learning the video surfaced, Kalanick was physically brought to his knees. Had he been caught yelling at anyone else, perhaps it wouldn't have been as damaging a moment for Kalanick. But "the driver" was Uber's central character. Employees had been told that their work mission was to make a driver's life more productive, lucrative, and happy. And yet the person who'd been waving that banner was now on film, berating their central character, screaming that some people don't "take responsibility for their own shit" and "they blame everything in their life on somebody else."[12] Over the following months top talent fled the company, Lyft (Uber's biggest competitor at the time) received a spike of funding from investors, and Kalanick was forced to resign.

If you were to look back at my original pitch deck for Rise, you'd see that I led with statements like "Dieting is a $30 billion industry, growing every year, and ripe for disruption." The more time I spent with investors, the further away I felt from my central character—the one person who led me to Rise in the first place.

I still remember the day my dad dropped me off at my middle school. We had agreed on a pickup spot for 3 p.m. After school, I waited there for what felt like hours, watching the Michigan sky turn uncharacteristically dark for early fall. By the time my aunt rushed into the parking lot to pick me up, my father was already on an operating table. Turns out, he had a doctor's appointment that morning, took a cardiology stress test, and collapsed.

Eight days after open-heart surgery, a different version of

my father was released from the hospital. He was in his forties but at times looked like he was in his eighties. We exited the hospital with a piece of paper titled "Behavior Modification," which had an alphabetized list of suggested foods for Dad's diet, beginning with "broccoli" and "Brussels sprouts." But we were an Indian family who ate Indian food—broccoli and Brussels sprouts weren't on the menu. And so began a multiyear struggle of watching my dad cycle through different diets, but none of them clicked. All the while doctors warned if we couldn't figure out one he could sustain, he would be back in the operating room—and soon.

Backable people helped me bring my central character into focus in the pitch room. I began to walk investors through my dad's story, from the day he was rushed to the operating room, to the months of unsuccessful dieting, to the day we met a nutritionist who would ultimately help turn his health around. Then, after going through the storyboard, I shared the numbers. While these were unsettling times in the Gupta household, we were by no means alone. Hundreds of thousands of patients undergo open-heart surgery every year, leaving the hospital with a similar behavior modification plan. One in five will be rehospitalized within sixty-five days of the operation. Then I zoomed investors out even further. Forty-five million Americans are actively dieting every year. The average dieter will try four times in a given year and fail—a $70 billion cycle that leads millions to frustration, depression, and heart failure.

This was the pitch that captivated attention—beginning with one person, my dad, and then showing just how many people share his struggle. A year after securing funding, I bumped into one of my lead investors at a cocktail party. She was in the middle of a conversation with a senior executive from Nordstrom. Perhaps to add some spark to the conversation, the Nordstrom executive asked my investor what inspired her to invest in Rise. My investor paused for a moment, then said, "His father's story. That really hit me."

STEP 3:

FIND AN EARNED SECRET

Years ago, I interviewed for a role with a fast-growing tech startup that had recently started making activity trackers to compete with the company Fitbit. My interview was with the CEO, and to prepare, I searched for information online. I read articles, watched videos, and jotted my thoughts down in a document. But the day before our sit-down, something struck me—everything I was about to share in the interview the CEO obviously already knew.

So I decided to try something else. I went to UserTesting.com, which lets you hire real human beings to test your product and give you feedback. I filled out a form asking people to try out the startup's website, and within a few hours I received three separate feedback videos. Combing through the footage, I noticed a pattern—while each of the testers seemed excited about the activity tracker's features, they all seemed to be confused on how to add the device to their shopping cart. It wasn't clear how to actually purchase the product.

The next morning, I walked into the interview not just with my standard research, but with a fresh insight I couldn't have found through a Google search. About halfway through the interview I mentioned the website-navigation issue to the CEO. He listened but, at first, seemed to brush off the suggestion. After all, he had teams of people working on the website. So I asked if I could show him something on my phone. He nodded, and I awkwardly walked around the long conference table.

Then I pulled up the first clip. There was confusion in this customer's voice: "I'm not exactly sure how to get from here to checkout." In the second clip, the customer seemed slightly more irritated. With a heavy sigh, she said, "Do I just need to reload the site and start again?" By the time we got to the last clip, the CEO was no longer staring at my screen, but rather at me.

"Where did you get these videos?" he asked. Turning to him, I explained that I had gathered them myself. He took a moment, then said, "I've interviewed hundreds of people—and no one's ever prepared something like this."

The reality is that "this" wasn't all that much extra effort. All in, it took around $50 and an hour of my time. And the insights I gathered weren't necessarily earth-shattering, but they showed that I put the effort in to find something non-obvious. Hours after the interview, I stared at a generous job offer along with a kind note from the CEO, and felt like I might have finally cracked the code on job interviews. I reflected on the many I had blown and how one simple act could have changed things—going beyond basic research and finding an insight I could genuinely call my own.

I didn't end up taking the job, launching my startup instead, but that lesson stuck with me. It wasn't until years later that

I heard venture capitalist Ben Horowitz, co-founder of Andreessen Horowitz, articulate this concept in a much clearer
way than I could. During a discussion with a group of interns,
someone raised the question: as an entrepreneur, how do you
get to an idea?

Horowitz responded that great ideas typically stem from an
"earned secret"—discovered by going out into the world and
"learning something that not a lot of other people know." He
used Airbnb, a company he'd backed nearly ten years earlier,
as an example.

Horowitz said that the rough idea of Airbnb didn't actually
sound that good. "Blow up an air mattress, stick it in your
apartment, and rent it out—what could possibly go wrong?"
he joked.[1] Yet what stood out to Horowitz was how the
co-founders arrived at the idea.

It wasn't from online research, but rather from personal
experience that led to a surprise insight. Brian Chesky and Joe
Gebbia, recent graduates from the Rhode Island School of
Design, had just moved to San Francisco without jobs. When
their landlord raised their rent, they needed a way to raise
some cash fast. That's when they heard that all the hotels in
the city were booked for an industrial design conference that
was coming to town. So they bought a few air mattresses and
charged guests $80 to crash on their floor. It worked—not only
did people pay to sleep on an air mattress, but when Chesky
advertised the offer nearly five hundred people responded.[2]
When Chesky pitched his idea to investors, he wasn't simply
sketching out a high-level market analysis. He was sharing a
non-obvious insight that sparked his idea and pulled him to
go deeper.

How you arrive at an idea can be as important and meaningful as the idea itself. I'll never forget the story of how James

Cameron first pitched Peter Chernin on *Titanic,* which at the time was the most expensive movie ever made. Chernin told me that if the movie had flopped, he would have lost his job as chairman and CEO of 20th Century Fox. What stood out to Chernin during the pitch was how deep Cameron had personally gone into the subject matter. For more than half the meeting they didn't even discuss the film, but rather the ship itself and the night it sank. Cameron's knowledge of the event was "nothing short of extraordinary," Chernin later told me. He was able to articulate the full schematic of the ship and moment-by-moment timeline of the disaster. These insights led Cameron to the theme of income inequality. In the movie, his Romeo and Juliet would come from very different economic backgrounds, which meant they'd be assigned to stay in different parts of the ship, and because of that have very different chances of survival. "It was the most memorable pitch I have ever been a part of," Chernin told me.

When I was preparing for my interview with the activity tracker CEO, watching user tests I had personally collected, I felt a little like Cameron taking dives under water to personally examine the shipwreck of the *Titanic.* And I felt a little like Chesky renting mattresses on his own living room floor. Since then, I've learned specific things you can do to earn your own secret.

GO BEYOND GOOGLE

When Sudhir Venkatesh showed up at Steven Levitt's office at the University of Chicago to begin his PhD research, he was a Grateful Dead groupie with "hair down to his ass."[3] He told Levitt he was interested in researching the economics of gangs. To most graduate students, that would include handing out surveys, running focus groups, and collating findings on a spreadsheet. No one would have expected Venkatesh to do what he did. He embedded himself for nearly seven years inside the Black Kings—one of Chicago's most ruthless gangs.[4]

When Venkatesh and I met years later for coffee at Northwestern University, he shared little bits of what he'd experienced—from attending the gang's leadership meetings to having the windows of his car shot out, and the hidden microeconomy he was able to uncover while living in the project. By putting himself inside his research, Venkatesh discovered that, for most gang members, selling drugs on the street corner paid less than working at McDonald's.

By the time we met, Venkatesh was already a rising star in the academic community. He was giving talks around the country to standing-room-only auditoriums, and his findings had been featured prominently in the bestselling book *Freakonomics*. But what made his story remarkable wasn't just what he found—it was *how he found it*. By embedding himself so deeply (and dangerously) into his subject, Venkatesh had challenged how the academic establishment looked at collecting research. Sitting behind a desk no longer felt good enough.

Years later, I was at Imagine Entertainment in Beverly Hills waiting to meet with Brian Grazer, whose productions include *Apollo 13*, *A Beautiful Mind*, and *Arrested Development*. Altogether, Grazer's movies and television shows have yielded more than 40 Academy Awards and 190 Emmys. In the waiting area, I was surrounded by people who seemed to be preparing to pitch Grazer on their new big idea.

I was there for a different reason—to figure out what makes an idea backable to a reputable Hollywood producer. And as I was escorted to a sunny conference room, I thought to myself,

"If I were pitching Brian Grazer today, what would it take to grab his attention and get him excited?"

So I posed the question to him. "You have a room full of people waiting to come in here and pitch you. What's the single best piece of advice that would help them succeed?" Grazer paused for a moment, then said, "Give me something that isn't google-able. I want an idea that is based on a surprise insight. Not something I could find through a Google search."

Sensing that I could use an example, Grazer gave me one, going into pitch mode himself. "Did you know in Atlanta, Georgia there was a high school that every single rapper came out of? Andre 3000, Big Boi came out of it…out of this one high school…did you know that?" I didn't know that, and Grazer immediately had my attention. I wanted to hear more.

Brian Grazer and Ben Horowitz look at different types of ideas in different industries, but as it turns out, they're essentially looking for the same thing. They're looking for a Sudhir Venkatesh—someone who has gone way deeper than Google. Someone who has personally put themselves inside the story and uncovered something that most people don't know.

Again, how you arrive at an idea can be as memorable and important as the idea itself. During a trip to Zimbabwe, Logan Green noticed that the locals had created a network of shared ride vans, referred to as Kombis, to get around given the lack of public transportation and the fact that very few people could afford a car. Green was so enamored with the system that he decided to personally bring something like it back to his neighborhood in California, where the roads were getting increasingly congested. He named the service Zimride after

Zimbabwe, and became one of the company's first drivers. When I asked investor Ann Miura-Ko what got her interested in Zimride, she told me that Green "didn't dance on the edges. He went inside the idea." Miura-Ko loved that Green personally carted passengers around the Los Angeles area and collected firsthand feedback during each ride.[5] She went on to become the first investor in Zimride, which eventually changed its name to Lyft.

Similarly, I remember when a filmmaker friend of mine called me, really excited about a new documentary he was working to help get off the ground. It was a film about how Wisconsin flipped from Democratic to Republican in the 2016 election. I knew he had looked at other ideas with the same theme and asked him what stood out about this one. He said, "They actually moved from California to Wisconsin to figure out what happened."

So when you're sharing the insight that led you to your idea, ask yourself, *Is this google-able?* If it is, then take your research deeper. Set up interviews with experts, take a trip, join a nonprofit that's relevant to your idea. If you're interested in cryptocurrency, don't just read a report; set up an account and start making trades. If you're interested in autonomous vehicles, don't just subscribe to a newsletter; visit a factory, drive a car. If you're interested in cannabis, well…in a growing number of states you now have options.

Go beyond Google. That's where the secrets lie.

INTOXICATE THEM WITH EFFORT

Once you've gone beyond Google, make sure your pitch demonstrates your effort. Don't share just your idea, but the effort as well—the work you did in the field that brought you to it. This might sound obvious, but it's often missed.

A few months ago I was introduced to an automotive executive who was about to pitch a proposal for the second time to senior management, and the initial rejection had gotten inside his head. "I'm stammering through my slides, and I don't stammer," he told me over the phone. I suggested he practice in front of someone who could help him feel more at ease. "I've been practicing in front of my wife," he replied. "It's just getting worse."

We decided to meet at a quiet coffee shop outside Detroit. When he walked me through his presentation, it was one of the more comprehensive pitches I had seen. He had completely broken down the supply chain for one of the automotive components his company produced and had methodically demonstrated choke points in the process that were costing the company tens of millions of dollars a year. It seemed like a home run, yet he came off as hesitant and unsure. I wanted to understand why. "You mentioned that you collected data from the field," I said. "How did you find it?" He nervously flipped to slide 8 to show me a financial model, but I asked him to step back from his keyboard for a moment. "*How* did you collect that data?" Puzzled by my question, he responded, "I'm not sure what you mean. I went to the factory, observed the processes, and did the numbers."

"Okay, can you tell me more about your visits to the factory?" I asked. As it turned out, he had been visiting the assembly line nearly every day, almost entirely on his own time, early in the mornings or after work. He would huddle together with the factory floor workers to diagram out options for a more efficient process. After several months of this, he knew each line worker by name and had gotten to know one of the supervisors so well that he was attending his son's birthday party the following weekend. While explaining all this, his stammers had completely stopped. He spoke with confidence about what he'd observed and genuine empathy for the people his proposed process could help.

His original presentation—the one that was rejected—laid out all the data but skipped all his personal legwork. How he had gone beyond his desk—beyond Google—on his own watch, with his own initiative. All the time he spent at the factory was a footnote when it should have been a sub-headline. For all his audience knew, he had come to his ideas by making a few phone calls and crunching some numbers.

We spent the rest of our time at the coffee shop reworking his presentation. We didn't change a single slide—only the narrative he used to describe his recommendations. For example, when he displayed the data for a bottleneck at one of the stations, we added a snippet of how he personally observed the choke point during his factory visits. "Lisa, who's been on the line for the past eight years, pointed this out to me while we were examining a conveyor together."

His big presentation took place the following Monday morning. That night, he forwarded me an email from one of the team's senior leaders green-lighting his proposal. It concluded with, "By the way, amazing presentation. I've got one coming up and wonder if I could run it by you."

An idea that stems from hands-on experience is way more backable than the same exact idea if it simply originated sitting behind a desk. But the catch is, without being boastful, you have to make that effort shine through your pitch. It can't be hidden.

Jonathan Karp is the CEO of book publisher Simon & Schuster. Karp worked his way up the publishing industry, from editorial assistant to editor-in-chief, collaborating with marquee names like Bruce Springsteen and Mario Puzo. But there was one name he had been pursuing, unsuccessfully, for almost twelve years: Howard Stern.

Karp shared with me that he had grown up listening to *The Howard Stern Show* and thought there was a real story of how the radio host had personally evolved. But Stern, who already had two bestsellers under his belt, didn't see the point of adding yet another book to the list. The process had been "torture" for Stern, a perfectionist who obsessed about the details, and he didn't want to have to live up to the success of his previous books.[6] Besides, he had a full-time job and didn't feel like spending the time and energy required for a new book. During those twelve years, Karp tried everything to change his mind. He wrote letters, sent books, and dined with Don Buchwald, Stern's agent. Nothing worked. "Stern turned into my white whale," he told me.

So, after a decade of rejection, Karp shifted tactics. Karp's vision for the book had essentially been a collection of transcripts from existing interviews between Stern and his most notable guests. That meant most of the work was already done. But rather than making that argument to Stern, Karp decided to roll up his sleeves and show him.

Along with Sean Manning, a newly hired editor, Karp combed through hundreds of Stern's interviews, over a million words' worth of transcripts, to extract the most bookworthy moments. All this was highly unusual hands-on work for the head of a major publishing house, but Karp wasn't finished.

He pulled the edited transcripts into a beautiful cloth-bound book with a polished-looking jacket, high-resolution images, and an organized table of contents. Then, instead of giving Stern another pitch to write a book, he sent Stern the actual book. Along with the product, Karp included a note. "This will be easy. You won't have to do any work." All Stern needed to do was add some personal reflections and, with that, the book would be done.

It turned out to be real work for Stern, but seeing the book ultimately convinced him to invest the time and energy required to take over and fully author the project. He later described Karp's approach as intoxicating. "Surely no one in the history of publishing had ever gone to so much trouble to get a dude to write a book."[7] The trouble was worth it. Upon release, *Howard Stern Comes Again* jumped to the top of the *New York Times* bestseller list.

You might be wondering, as I did, why the underlying effort makes such a difference if the idea is the same. After all, the automotive executive's recommendation to the senior executives didn't change. And Karp's vision for the book had remained the same. But with above-and-beyond effort, they were able to show dedication and drive. They were able to tell a more exciting story, with characters and visuals. When people see that you're so embedded in an idea, it also makes it harder for them to say no. Remember a key part of what intrigued Ben Horowitz about Airbnb was that Brian Chesky personally threw himself into the problem he wanted to solve. A key part of what intrigued the *Freakonomics* authors about Sudhir Venkatesh was that he personally experienced his research. Just like Karp, they went beyond Google and then wove that effort into their story. *How* we arrive at an idea can be just as important as the idea itself.

I didn't fully realize this until a late August afternoon when I was inside a Palo Alto conference room pitching an investor on Rise. Though the last few investors had been a "hard pass,"

I walked in optimistic because this particular investor had a strong interest in healthcare. But within the first few minutes I began to see all the signals of a bored backer. He didn't ask me anything, his nodding was on autopilot, and every time I asked if he had questions, he shot back with a "No, I'm good."

When he picked up his phone and started typing in the middle of my pitch, I knew I was done. I thought about ending early, but that would be poor form. Besides, I needed the practice. But as I jumped to the next slide, his assistant popped her head inside the conference room and said something along the lines of "Your four p.m. is here early." When he picked up his phone earlier, I wondered if he'd actually been texting her, "Get me the hell out of here. Please."

As she left the room, he collected his phone and unopened notebook and started to get up from his seat. "Hey, I'm sorry," he said. "We're in the middle of closing a deal and I need to hop." As he started for the door, he looked at the slide on the screen one last time. The headline of the slide was "Pilot Program" and the data on the slide showed a breakdown of the customers who had participated in our initial test. Perhaps because he felt bad for leaving early, he decided to ask one last question. "How did you find your customers for your pilot program?"

It wasn't a question I liked to be asked, because the answer was unimpressive. But this investor was already a clear "pass," and I wasn't even sure if he was paying attention, so I blurted it out. "I stood outside Weight Watchers meetings."

He looked up from his phone, surprised.

"What?" he said in a way that made me immediately regret sharing that story. But now it was already out there. "I . . . stood outside Weight Watchers meetings. As people arrived, I asked them if I could show them a quick demo. That's how we found our first customers."

"You found your first customers standing outside Weight Watchers?" he asked. I nodded.

Now I really regretted giving him the unimpressive answer. He was clearly taken aback by my amateurishness. I imagined him at happy hour later that day with his group of drinking buddies—probably also investors—telling this story, fighting to get the words out between belly laughs. There I was, trying to portray myself as a cutting-edge, innovative CEO. Instead he saw me as someone on a street corner spinning a large cardboard sign to promote half-price turkey subs.

Defeated, I began to close my laptop and pack up my stuff. "Hang on," he said. "Do you have a few more minutes?"

His question puzzled me. "Sure," I said.

He sat back down and, for the first time in our meeting, put his phone not on the table, but in his pocket. "Can you start from the top on the pilot program?" he asked. So I did. Only this time I didn't gloss over *how* we found our pilot customers. I shared all the details of my half-baked strategy standing in front of different Weight Watchers locations and pitching customers before they walked through the door. I told him how one Weight Watchers location had me removed from the premises. And how I accidentally approached someone who, as it turned out, wasn't a Weight Watchers member. The investor hadn't cracked a smile during our entire time together. Now he was laughing out loud.

In the middle of all this, his assistant poked her head back into our room. She was clearly confused by the laughter and the fact that he was still talking to me. The investor turned to her and said, "I'm going to need a while." A few days later, he offered to invest.

STEP 4:

MAKE IT FEEL INEVITABLE

Adam Lowry and his business partner, Eric Ryan, had $300,000 in credit card debt and only $16 in their startup's bank account. Vendors refused to give them any more product until they paid their bills. They needed a backer for their new designer soap company, but the economy was in a hole, consumer products were out of vogue, and the founders had zero track record in this space. Lowry's most recent professional pursuit included trying out for, and not making, the Olympic sailing team. All this made his pitch for funding close to impossible.

So I thought it was strange when Lowry told me he didn't take a pitch deck to his first pitch meeting. Instead, he presented his first investor with a trend book.

Inside were clipped photos from Restoration Hardware, Williams-Sonoma, and Waterworks—all brands that had emerged as unlikely winners since the economy had hit a downturn. With the burst of the bubble came a return to the nest. People who previously bought furniture from department stores were looking to a new crop of exclusive home stores to curate their living spaces. This trend in consumer behavior was so pronounced it gave rise to a new segment of media publications focused on the home, including magazines like *Wallpaper*, *Dwell*, and *Real Simple*.

A typical pitch communicates that an idea is new. Lowry's pitch communicated that his idea was *inevitable*. People were already choosing to style their living rooms and bedrooms—it was only a matter of time before this trend reached bathrooms and kitchens. To get ahead of the curve, Lowry was designing a cleaning product that you'd be proud to leave on the kitchen counter when guests were around. Lowry's designer soap would come in bright, candy-paint colors that smelled like cucumber and mandarin orange and yuzu. They were packaged in a clear and cool-looking bottle dreamed up by Karim Rashid, a top-notch industrial designer.

Lowry's message to investors was simple—the market is already moving in this direction. Join me and we'll ride this wave together. It worked; Lowry raised money from reputable investors who believed in the inevitability of a soap brand called Method.

BE AN ARMCHAIR ANTHROPOLOGIST

Tina Sharkey has spent the past twenty-five years creating and selling backable ideas. Early in her career, she built the consumer brand iVillage, which caught the attention of the executives who recruited her to launch the digital division inside Sesame Workshop. She later worked at AOL and headed up BabyCenter. When I asked Sharkey how she successfully wore so many hats in her career, she pointed to the one that mattered most, what she refers to as her "cultural anthropologist hat."

Sharkey says this role starts with a question: "What is the *shift* in the world that is making your idea matter?" Before jumping to the description of her solution, she puts on her anthropologist hat to figure out how the world is changing. Then she fits her idea into this larger shift.

At first, this seemed a little backward to me. If my goal was to pitch a specific idea, then why would I waste a backer's time with such a macro perspective? But as I interviewed backable people from all walks of life—inside big companies and small—I realized how every one of them took on the role of an "armchair anthropologist" and first showed investors where the world was headed. To expand BabyCenter from a web service to a robust mobile product, Sharkey first showed how moms had already made the shift—even if advertising dollars hadn't. To pitch Method, Lowry showed how people were beginning to style every aspect of their home, even the parts that were out of sight. To pitch Airbnb, the founders showed how the idea of "sharing your home with a stranger" had changed from creepy to widely accepted. Slide 4 of Airbnb's original pitch deck read:

- 630,000 listings on couchsurfing.com
- 17,000 temporary housing listings on SF & NYC Craigslist[1]

Backable people seem to always be acting as anthropologists, looking for trends and changes. For Jennifer Hyman, her anthropological find came when her sister showed her a new dress she'd bought. The price tag read $2,000. Hyman knew her sister couldn't afford that kind of expense—it was sending her into credit card debt—and asked her why she didn't simply wear one of her other dresses to the friend's wedding.[2] Clearly, there was a dress in her closet that people hadn't seen before, right? Wrong. Hyman's sister was active on social media, which meant that anyone at the wedding who followed her on Facebook would know that she wore the same dress twice. To avoid that, she was more than willing to max out her credit card.

That's when Hyman realized that a shift was happening—the increasing pressure of social media was ballooning wardrobe budgets, for many to unhealthy levels. With that anthropological insight, Hyman put on her creator hat to find a solution. She came up with the idea for a service that allowed women to rent dresses for special occasions—like a Netflix for high-end clothing.[3] She called it Rent the Runway. When Hyman presented her creation to audiences and backers, she didn't go straight to the solution, but started with the shift.

Had she jumped straight into the solution—a service that rents dresses to people who can't afford to own them outright—a backer may have wondered, why now? After all, designer dresses have always been expensive. Instead, Hyman walked backers through the shift she first noticed with her sister. Fashion-forward people who used to post weekly to social media were now posting daily. And they didn't want to double dip into the same outfit for their social media feed. With that shift in mind, dress rentals didn't seem like just a good idea; it seemed like an inevitable one. Investors backed the business with millions of dollars in funding, and today Rent the Runway has expanded to everyday clothes, accessories, and even home goods—anything that might appear on an Instagram feed.

*　　*　　*

When I started pitching Rise, I would skip the shift and jump straight into the solution. I would immediately show the app I wanted to build, the type of team I wanted to assemble, and the road map I needed to succeed. But because I missed a vital step, investors were left wondering why the world needed this now.

It wasn't the first time I made this mistake. In 2007, the year the iPhone was launched, I was working at Sony Pictures Television. Even though the iPhone was an infant, I believed the studio should start investing significant resources in creating content that would look good on a mobile-size screen. But when I pitched the senior team, I skipped the shift and jumped straight to the solution. My slide deck included examples of snack-size storylines, designs for what these would look like on an iPhone, and financial projections for the overall project. But I never made the case that the iPhone was going to inevitably change everything, or that the industry would inevitably make a shift toward mobile content. As a result, the executives missed the larger context and my pitch came off looking like a pet project. When we got to financial projections, one executive shouted, "That profit wouldn't pay for lunch on today's set!" Maybe he would have felt different had I demonstrated the macro trends first. Record labels had perilously ignored the iPod, and we didn't want to make the same mistake with the iPhone. But because I didn't make a strong case for what was already happening and what would inevitably happen, my solution felt unnecessary.

Though I made the mistake of leaving my anthropologist hat behind, Adam Lowry never really took his off. After selling Method, he spotted another lifestyle shift. More and more people were beginning to follow a "flexitarian diet," or what author Michael Pollan prescribes as "Eat food. Not too much. Mostly plants." Just as Lowry followed the inevitable expansion from styling the living room to styling the cupboard, he followed the trajectory of plant-based foods to plant-based milk.

When Lowry walked backers through his new idea, he followed the same playbook he'd used for Method and began with the shift. He explained that it used to be that only lactose-intolerant customers purchased dairy-alternative products, but now more than 85 percent of nondairy-milk customers were not lactose intolerant.[4] "They bought it because they wanted to, not because they had to, and they weren't going to sacrifice taste or nutrition," he said.

Just as with Method, Lowry explained the macro trend to investors, then introduced them to Ripple, a new plant-based milk with the same level of protein as regular milk. Ripple went on to raise nearly $100 million in funding and is now sold in Whole Foods and Target stores across the United States.

WITH OR WITHOUT US

Daniel Kahneman won a Nobel Prize for helping the world understand how we make decisions. One of the key underpinnings of Kahneman's contribution is what scientists call "loss aversion," which suggests that, psychologically, the pain of losing is *twice* as powerful as the pleasure of gaining. Kahneman points out that most people will "reject a gamble in which they might lose $20, unless they are offered more than $40 if they win."[5]

Loss aversion can help us understand a lot about our colleagues, our friends, and ourselves. It helps us understand why a driver with no history of car accidents pays Avis extra for collision insurance. It helps us understand why someone holds on to a downward-trending stock so that the paper loss doesn't turn into an actual loss.

And it can also explain why backers are reluctant to invest in anything that doesn't feel safe. Even venture capitalists who look for risky investments turn down the overwhelming majority of new ideas they hear. Instagram, Facebook, and Amazon were rejected by multiple investors. A well-respected venture capitalist once told me, "If I said no to 100 percent of the ideas I hear, I'd be right 99 percent of the time."

If the fear of betting on the wrong idea is twice as powerful as the pleasure of betting on the right idea, then we can't neutralize the fear of losing with the pleasure of winning. We can only neutralize the fear of losing with...the fear of losing.

Enter FOMO, the fear of missing out. For backers, the only thing equally powerful to missing is...missing out. No one wants to be the Hollywood studio that passed on *Star Wars,* the university that rejected Albert Einstein, or the executive at Blockbuster who passed on buying Netflix for $50 million.[6] (Today, Blockbuster is out of business, and Netflix has surpassed a valuation of $200 billion.)

We see FOMO play out everywhere. Once a founder has a lead investor, other investors want to join the round. Once an employee has a competing job offer, he or she is much more likely to receive a raise. Once a real estate agent has an offer, he's more likely to attract other offers.

FOMO is so powerful that it can inspire entire industries. Autonomous vehicles have existed for more than fifty years but have become a strategic priority for every major automaker thanks to FOMO. In 1962, General Motors showcased its

Firebird III,[7] featuring an "electronic guide system [that] can rush it over an automatic highway while the driver relaxes."[8] Ford Motor Company was working on its own self-driving initiatives around this time.

But decades later, when Silicon Valley companies like Google and Apple entered the autonomous-vehicle game, Ford and GM advanced autonomous vehicles from an R&D project to a strategic imperative. GM struck first, acquiring a self-driving startup called Cruise Automation for more than $1 billion.[9] Dripping with FOMO, other automakers followed suit. Ford announced a $1 billion investment[10] in a four-month-old startup named Argo AI, Fiat Chrysler partnered with Google's self-driving division Waymo,[11] and Mercedes partnered with Uber to produce a fleet of autonomous vehicles.[12] Both Ford and GM opened up large Silicon Valley offices to ensure the other didn't have exclusive access to top technical talent. In a matter of months, FOMO took the autonomous vehicle space from zero to sixty.

As creators, our job isn't to use FOMO to manipulate backers, but rather to neutralize their fear of taking a bad bet. Though it may sound strange, FOMO can make a risky bet feel safe because it shields us from the risk of being left behind. This feeling of inevitability rarely comes from the argument that we should change the world, but rather from the argument that the world is already changing—with or without us.

Some time after I botched my iPhone pitch at Sony Pictures Television, Sam Schwartz gave a masterclass-worthy pitch inside Comcast. As the head of business development, Schwartz told me that he wanted to convince the rest of senior management that they needed to launch a mobile service so that Comcast could serve the customer both inside and outside the home.

Unlike me, Schwartz didn't make the case that his mobile service *should* happen. He made the case that it was already happening. Schwartz pointed to Europe, which was consistently five years ahead of the United States on mobile trends, and already bundling wired with wireless. He also revealed that AT&T and Verizon were showing signs of doing the same in the United States. If Comcast didn't move fast, it would be left behind. By getting everyone to agree with the shift, Schwartz was able to glide into presenting his solution: Xfinity Mobile.

Counterintuitively, showing that change is inevitable means showing that your vision isn't necessarily unique—just slightly ahead. Adam Lowry demonstrated that cleaning products would inevitably become stylish home accessories, with or without Method. Sam Schwartz showed that inside-outside home integration would inevitably happen, with or without Comcast. Just as Jennifer Hyman showed that brands would inevitably shift from selling to renting, with or without Rent the Runway. Fast-forward to today, and they have. Within the next decade, clothing rental is expected to become a $40 billion industry with dozens of players, including traditional retailers such as Urban Outfitters and Banana Republic now offering this service.[13]

Tien Tzuo cut his teeth at Salesforce, in the Marc Benioff–inspired culture of "shift happens." As the company's first chief marketing officer, Tzuo got an anthropological view into how businesses were changing how they bought software. He followed what was happening and identified two major shifts. On the one hand, large iconic companies with long histories were completely disappearing. On the other hand, newer brands like Zipcar and Netflix were thriving through a business model powered by "subscriptions."

The deeper Tzuo went, the more he believed subscriptions

weren't just a tool for startups, but an inevitable trend for big companies that wanted to stay alive. He coined a term for the trend—"the subscription economy"—and created a new company, Zuora, to help companies take advantage of it. Today Zuora is a publicly traded company serving a range of established companies from Zoom to the *Guardian*.[14] Yet Tzuo's message to potential customers has remained consistent: this shift is going to happen with or without you. Do you want to come along or be left behind?

SHOW MOMENTUM

FOMO's blood brother is momentum. It's not enough to show that your idea is inevitable; you have to show that your idea is in forward motion. Momentum makes FOMO feel real. Without it, your case for inevitability can fall flat.

In 2017, Walmart acquired Bonobos for more than $300 million, but when Andy Dunn was first pitching the company in 2007, he struggled to find investors. At the time, only 7 percent of apparel was sold online, too little to demonstrate a significant business opportunity. Perhaps more of a blocker was the fact that Bonobos was selling "better-fitting pants," but the consumer couldn't even try them on before buying because they were fully online. There was skepticism that people would take a gamble on whether a pair of pants actually fit.

Instead of arguing against that logic, Dunn illustrated how things were changing. As an example, he pointed to the online shoe business, Zappos. "Investors initially didn't think that people would buy shoes online," Dunn would explain to skeptics. As with pants, they thought customers would demand to try them on first. And yet Zappos had become a fast-growing business, and Amazon would later purchase it for nearly $1 billion.[15] With his anthropologist hat on, Dunn made the case to himself and others that if shoes could sell online, then so could pants.

A sense of inevitability made investors believe in the concept of "Zappos meets Ralph Lauren," but it was momentum that made investors believe that Bonobos could be that brand. By the time they started raising funding, Dunn and his co-founder, Brian Spaly, had been selling out of the trunk of a car and at "pants parties" hosted at friends' apartments. While all this generated less than $100,000 in revenue, not enough to make a Silicon Valley investor swoon, it showed they were more than a PowerPoint deck. Without that early momentum, Dunn told me, "no one would have been interested."

You don't need a lot of momentum to create FOMO and show signs of inevitability. Bonobos pants were being sold out of Trader Joe's bags, Method was being distributed in only a handful of stores, and Rent the Runway was testing its concept in New York, New Haven, and Boston.[16] But these actions were enough to show that these were more than just ideas. Real action was being taken to ride the inevitable wave.

HAVE VISION, NOT VISIONS

WeWork was originally rooted in two massive, inevitable shifts. First, the freelance economy had exploded in size. In 2019, 57 million workers in the United States were members of the gig economy.[17] The socioeconomic shift toward freelancing had begun in the wake of the 2008 recession, prompting many new freelancers to go looking for a spare desk. Second, big companies were rapidly distributing their workforces. "Work from home" was becoming more commonplace, even before COVID-19 struck, and companies were beginning to set up satellite locations to access new pockets of talent.

Both of these trends played into WeWork's origin story. By the time they became the most valued startup in the U.S., at $47 billion,[18] freelancers and millennials constituted more than a third of the country's workforce.[19] At the time, there was high-fidelity clarity on where the world was headed and how WeWork fit in.

But then all of a sudden, the story began to blur in a big way. Adam Neumann, the startup's founder, announced that they would be expanding from co-working space to schools, local banking, and eventually shuttle visits to Mars. Backers were stunned by the new direction, priorities, and use of resources. The vision of the company no longer seemed based on where the world was going, but on where Neumann thought the world *should* go. When discussing Neumann, one investor told me that there is a difference between a founder who has vision and one who is having visions.

While Neumann's inner circle seemed to applaud the new vision, Wall Street felt differently when the company filed to go public. Among other issues, analysts didn't believe Neumann's plan was rooted in reality. As a result, the initial public offering was canceled, the company's valuation plummeted by billions of dollars, and thousands of people were laid off. Neumann was forced to resign and new leadership was brought in to bring The We Company back to its fundamentals.[20]

As I was writing this book, some people close to Neumann told me he was simply "doing what Steve Jobs would have done," by thinking differently and expansively. But it's easy to forget that the iPhone was inevitable and deeply rooted in reality. By the time it was launched in 2007, IBM had already launched a smartphone with a touchscreen, and more than 30 million people had bought a PalmPilot.[21] Nokia had also demo'd a touchscreen phone that could locate a restaurant, play a racing game, and order lipstick.

In 1994, *Wired* magazine covered General Magic, which was executing on designs that were almost identical to the original iPhone. When the startup ran out of money, two of its senior leaders—Tony Fadell and Andy Rubin—went to Apple and Google to lead the iPhone and Android. Some 99 percent of smartphones today can be attributed to those two product leaders who aren't Steve Jobs.[22]

But Jobs did accelerate what was already in motion. In his iPhone launch speech, he continuously made the point that the world had already been headed in the direction of the iPhone, and now...it was finally here. He concluded his remarks with, "There's an old Wayne Gretzky quote that I love. 'I skate to where the puck is going to be.'"

As I struggled to get Rise off the ground, I watched Jobs's speech over and over again. While backable people like Tina Sharkey had taught me the importance of relating my idea to an inevitable shift in the hearts and minds of people, it was watching Jobs on YouTube that inspired me to pay attention to where the puck was headed in the world of healthcare.

What I saw was an inevitable change in the way medical practitioners were communicating—doctors emailing with patients, nurses corresponding over video, and orthopedic surgeons viewing medical images on their phones. Our entire way of communicating with medical practitioners was shifting from low-frequency, in-person visits to higher-frequency, remote check-ins.

And while most of these engagements were happening over video, I came to the conclusion that practitioners and patients would inevitably be communicating via text messages and photos. I began to walk investors through this natural evolution, citing the rise of SMS frequency, particularly among senior citizens. Only after establishing this trend line did I introduce them to my idea: a service where you take photos of your food and get instant text-based feedback from a personal nutritionist.

STEP 5:

FLIP OUTSIDERS TO INSIDERS

We've been told that creativity is a two-step formula: a great idea plus great execution. But there is a "secret step" in between. This is where you turn outsiders into insiders so that when your idea reaches the execution stage you arrive together. Nearly every great movement, organization, and campaign can be traced back to this secret step.

In the 1940s, "instant cake mixes" were unveiled at grocery stores across the United States with lots of marketing and hype. All you needed to prepare a tasty dessert was to add water, pour the batter in a pan, and bake. It took less than half the time and effort of making a cake from scratch. So marketers were stunned to find that their product wasn't selling.

It took a psychologist named Ernest Dichter to figure out why. After cross-examining homemakers across the country, Dichter came to a shocking conclusion: the mixes made cooking *too* easy. They all but removed the consumer from the creative process. So manufacturers tried something new—they removed the egg from the mix, requiring you to crack and mix one in yourself. Sales took off.[1]

In the coming decades, researchers would see this pattern over and over again. Michael Norton from Harvard Business School, along with two colleagues, eventually named it "the IKEA effect"[2] and demonstrated that we place nearly five times more value on a product we helped build than on a product we simply buy. "Time spent touching objects" leads to "feelings of ownership and value."[3]

Could a backer feel that sense of ownership for someone else's idea? At first, I didn't see the connection, which is why I'd walk into pitches trying my best to show I had a thorough plan, with every major and minor detail figured out. I believed my ideas needed to be bulletproof in order to be backable.

But as I continued to bring ideas to backers, I realized something—the more pinned down my plan, the less enthusiasm I was able to generate. My best pitches tended to be the ones with at least one open question, which I posed to the room. Those meetings would begin with the backers on the opposite side of the table and typically end with us huddled around my laptop or phone, working through something together. Through these experiences, I stumbled into a somewhat hidden lesson for being backable: we tend to fight the hardest for ideas for which we feel some sense of ownership.

Why does that matter? Because even if a backer likes your idea, they almost always have to still convince someone else. If a venture capitalist likes your startup, they will likely need to sell it to the rest of their partners. If the CEO of your company likes your idea for a new product, they still might need to share it with their board. If an editor likes your book concept, they still need to convince a committee to make an offer.

That's why when we pitch, we're not looking for just a backer; we're looking for an advocate. Someone who can represent your idea with the same enthusiasm as you. Salman Rushdie once wrote, "Most of what matters in our lives takes place in our absence."[4] While we're present for the pitch, we're most likely absent for the hallway huddles, backroom meetings, and email threads that decide the fate of our ideas. Backers become fierce advocates when they are on the inside of an idea. They crack their own egg and add it to the mix.

After wrapping up *An Inconvenient Truth,* documentary film-maker Davis Guggenheim decided to shift his focus from climate change to a personal passion—the electric guitar. His idea was to create a film profiling the biggest guitarists of all time. At the very top of his wish list was perhaps the greatest of them all—Led Zeppelin's Jimmy Page.

When Guggenheim ran the idea by his team, the consensus was universal: it will never happen. "Bringing Jimmy Page into the film would have been a dream," Guggenheim told me. "But none of us believed we could get him. He was too private." In fact, in Page's fifty-plus-year career, he'd given only a handful of interviews—none of which were at the depth required for a feature-length documentary film.

Guggenheim pressed on, eventually finding his way to Page's business manager, who confirmed everyone's doubts. When Guggenheim asked for an opportunity to personally share the idea with Page, the manager said, "I'll give you an hour," not expecting that Guggenheim would take a ten-hour flight from Los Angeles to London for a short meeting. But Guggenheim booked one of the first flights he could find to Heathrow.

He met Page in the lobby of a London hotel where the two talked over English tea. From the moment they sat down, the pressure was on Guggenheim to convince the rock and roll icon to do something he'd never done before. Perhaps Page might have been expecting a hard sell. But it never came.

"Jimmy, I don't know what this film is going to be...but let's tell this story together. Why don't we start with a casual conversation? No cameras. Just a microphone and no commitments. We'll just talk and see where it goes from there. At any minute, you can get up and leave." Guggenheim describes that moment as the turning point for the film. "I get it," Page responded. "It will be organic."

Guggenheim and Page rented a space at a small, local hotel and ended up talking for three days. As promised, there was no agenda or camera crew—just two human beings openly sharing ideas, reflections, and anecdotes. What emerged was the start of a film called *It Might Get Loud,* which was nominated for awards and hailed as "a triumphant and truly absorbing 90-minute spectacle."[5]

For me, Guggenheim's story represented a career-defining lesson. Bring the people you are counting on into your creative process so that they feel like co-owners of your idea. Even if it feels uncomfortable, don't be afraid to let people put their fingerprints on your projects. Make them an insider and they'll feel invested in your success. Tommy Harper, who has produced big-budget films like *Star Wars: The Force Awakens,* put it to me like this: "If they feel like it's their idea, then we all win."

SHARE WHAT IT COULD BE, NOT HOW IT HAS TO BE

Joel Stein is an author and former writer for *Time* magazine. Living in New York and Los Angeles, he eventually crossed into the entertainment scene and began to pitch ideas for television shows. Stein told me about the time he pitched CBS on a sitcom about a thirty-five-year-old indie rock star and drug addict. Before Stein went into his formal pitch, he and the executives made small talk about what inspired the idea. "In a world where adults watch Disney movies and eat cupcakes," Stein said casually, "recovering addicts are the only people who are trying to grow up." This sparked a lively discussion about our unpreparedness for true adulthood, giving Stein a perfect segue to his pitch—the story of his indie rock star addict.

Moments after Stein left the meeting, before he even reached his car, he received a call letting him know that CBS wanted to buy the show. But there was a catch. "They didn't want to buy my pitch," Stein told me. "They wanted to buy everything I said *before* the pitch." As it turned out, CBS wasn't interested in the thirty-five-year-old rock star plot, but they were very interested in the angle of "trying to grow up." They wanted to work with Stein on a different direction to take the same theme. So they bought the show—without buying the plot he authored—for more money than Stein's annual salary at *Time* magazine.

Had Stein gone straight into his formal pitch, the result might have been different. But the pre-pitch discussion invited the executives into the creative process. And almost by accident, Stein learned one of the cardinal rules of backability: share what it could be, but not exactly how it has to be.

Like Stein, I stumbled into this lesson by accident. My interpretation of a backable idea had been a bulletproof plan, with all the fine points figured out. But what I realized is that while it's important to have thought through all the details, you don't need to share them all in advance. Instead share the high-level theme of what the idea could be, then pause and bring your backers into the discussion.

A startup pitch deck typically has a "backup" section. These are slides that can be referenced after the initial pitch and during discussion. When I first started pitching Rise, only 10 percent of my overall deck was in the backup section. After backable people helped me reshape my deck, over 50 percent of my deck was in the backup section. Instead of sharing all of the details up front, I'd share the high-level idea and vision—then open it up to discussion. As a result, each pitch began to feel less like a presentation and more like a collaboration.

This is how Steve Jobs recruited a marketing consultant named Regis McKenna to shape the original brand identity for Apple. Jobs loved the work McKenna did on the Intel ads and wanted him to work on his logo. The problem was that Apple was an unknown brand and McKenna already had a stable of large, established clients.[6]

And yet within five minutes of meeting Jobs, McKenna decided to work with Apple. Why? Because instead of boring McKenna with a detailed set of specifications, essentially telling him exactly what Apple was, Jobs spoke passionately about what the brand *could be*. And it was the "what is possible talk" that invited McKenna into the process, not as a contributor, but as a collaborator and an insider.[7] As a result, he not only designed Apple's logo but helped construct the company's first business plan.[8]

While writing this book, I was introduced to Jonathan Dotan, who isn't your typical Hollywood screenwriter. He was originally hired by the creators of HBO's *Silicon Valley* as a technical consultant to make sure the show remained credible to their early-adopter audience—tech geeks who loved shows about tech geeks. During an episode, if even a single detail wasn't rooted in reality, it would lead to outrage on Reddit. Dotan, who had a unique mix of technical design and film experience, was brought on to fact-check and pressure-test each plot point to ensure it was technically rooted in reality.

In the season one finale, the writers wanted their main character, Richard Hendrix, to come up with a programming breakthrough—something that made his startup's compression algorithm exponentially better than anyone else's. A tall order for a tiny startup.

Dotan's job was to research and bring concepts into the writers' room, which can feel a lot like a Backable WrestleMania. Ideas are being thrown out from different directions, most of which drop on the floor. The pace is fast, the wit is sharp, and the voices are loud. You're lucky to have the room's attention, let alone its enthusiasm.

Dotan got to work on researching compression engines and found something that surprised him. The algorithms that power a lot of the consumer technology we use today haven't significantly changed for decades. This was an interesting enough insight that Dotan could have attempted to formulate and steer the writers toward his own specific plot line. Instead, he simply shared his discovery. "I didn't want to be prescriptive. I wanted to open up a conversation," Dotan later told me. During the writers' meeting, he walked the room through the two existing types of compression—top-down and bottom-up—and then added, "There hasn't been any real advancement since the 1970s." That was enough to rev up the creative horsepower of Mike Judge and Alec Berg, the two head writers. After reflecting on Dotan's presentation, they said to him, "You mentioned top-down and bottom-up. What about middle-out?"

Over the following weeks, Dotan and the writers collaborated on inventing and validating a brand-new type of compression engine. "Middle-out" became the capstone plot point for a show that won five Emmy nominations, earned the trust of a core audience of techies, and even inspired some viewers to build an actual startup based on the new compression engine.[9]

As for Dotan, he was able to play a key role in closing out a television season. He did so without ever trying to force his own idea. Had he burst into the room with a specific solution, the writers might never have arrived at the middle-out engine. Instead he shared the high level of what the idea could be, not how it had to be.

THE STORY OF US

Most great political speeches include three stories: the "story of me," "the story of you," and most important, the "story of us"—what happens when we join forces and work together. John F. Kennedy's inaugural speech masterfully did this when he laid out a bold agenda and then challenged people everywhere to ask what "together we can do for the freedom of man."[10]

I've discovered that founders often tell the "story of me," occasionally tell the "story of you," and almost never tell the "story of us." They tend to miss the opportunity to tell a backer why she is a specific fit for the idea, more than any other backer. When we miss this part of the story, we lose the chance to turn an outsider into an insider.

John Palfrey is head of the MacArthur Foundation, which awards a $625,000 grant every year to twenty or so people who, among other qualities, display "extraordinary originality and dedication in their creative pursuits." Over the past forty years the "genius grant," as it's commonly referred to, has been given to people like Chimamanda Ngozi Adichie, Tim Berners-Lee, and Lin-Manuel Miranda.

So I was surprised when Palfrey told me that if someone already has a clear path to success, that might make them a *weaker* candidate for the grant. He says a candidate is the strongest when they pass the "but for" test. "We look to support someone where, 'but for' our support, they wouldn't be able to accomplish their full potential," says Palfrey.

We see the same filter used by other selective programs. Stanford University's Graduate School of Business receives thousands upon thousands of applications every year and accepts only a few hundred students.[11] When I spoke to an admissions officer, he told me that most applications are simply a list of accomplishments. But the best applications show an intersection between your "gaps" and the program's strengths. In other words, they have a clear answer to: How do Stanford's unique strengths play into where you need to grow? Interestingly, the same type of analysis is used by the Aspen Institute's Henry Crown Fellowship Program, which has awarded fellowships to people like Senator Cory Booker and Netflix CEO Reed Hastings. One of the criteria for the fellowship is that the candidates be at an inflection point in their career. They must "not be fully-baked."[12]

Backable people taught me that there are three steps to showing backers they are a pivotal part of your plan.

First, identify a gap in your idea that relates directly to a strength in your backer. A gap could be anything from needing to figure out the right marketing strategy to hiring the right people. Months ago, a dermatologist approached me for fundraising advice so he could turn his one clinic into a chain. The biggest gap in his idea wasn't on the medical side, but on the retail side. Up until that point, he'd been approaching other physicians, with little success, to invest in his service. We shifted his fundraising strategy and began to approach investors with a retail background. That allowed him to tell the "story of us"—his medical expertise plus their retail expertise. That was a winning combination they wanted to fund.

Second, learn as much as possible before your meeting. Although you will be highlighting a gap, you still want to be able to engage your backer with the right questions and discussion. This takes preparation. In fact, I've learned it takes *more* preparation to create a discussion than to create a presentation.

Had the dermatologist approached retail investors with something like "I don't understand retail," that would have been a turnoff. Instead, he spent weeks learning everything he could about retail strategy. He called friends with relevant backgrounds, attended an online retail seminar, and spoke to shop owners in his neighborhood. In the days before the meeting, he came up with thoughtful options for a strategy. Again, he didn't shrug his shoulders and point to his own gap. He showed the work he'd already done in trying to figure it out and engaged the retail-expert investor in a discussion.

Finally, when you meet with your backer, be sure to directly express the "story of us." Explain how your gap and their strength fit together to unlock your idea. Don't assume that they'll connect the dots. Even if they do, it's worth them knowing that you understand why you two fit well together. In emails to potential investors, this dermatologist would emphasize how "your retail background" and "my clinical background" could be a nice fit. Not only did that set the relationship up with a collaborative tone; it also showed investors that he had done his research—and wasn't simply sending a template email to every investor he could find.

Emily Weiss, creator of the beauty blog *Into the Gloss,*

brought these steps together wisely when she was introduced to investor Kirsten Green, the Dollar Shave Club investor with the "Midas touch" we met earlier.[13] At the time, *Into the Gloss* had reached significant page views per month, and Weiss envisioned expanding the business in several ways, one of which included the potential for a physical product.[14] She clearly understood how to build and retain a loyal following but didn't know as much about how to build a product.[15] Green, on the other hand, had a strong retail background and had backed consumer product companies like Birchbox, Warby Parker, and Serena & Lily.[16]

Weiss fused her gap with Green's strength and deftly told the "story of us." Instead of preparing a formal pitch for Green, she talked about what she observed from readers of *Into the Gloss*, what they craved, and her various ideas on how she could deliver what they wanted. In her meeting with Green, she laid out those options, which immediately pulled the investor into the conversation about how they could build an online beauty brand. After an engaging discussion on the trade-offs of each, Weiss and Green decided the right initial go-to-market products were makeup and skin care. Today, Glossier, valued at $1.2 billion,[17] has added clothing, body care products, and fragrances to its lineup and has been called "one of the most disruptive brands in beauty" by *Fortune*.[18]

MAKE *THEM* THE HERO

Years ago, I came across a designer named Michelle who was incredibly in demand within her company. People would fight to have her on their team. I later discovered that while people liked Michelle's creativity, they loved her process even more.

After sharing a set of design options, Michelle always gathered input from the room. Then, in a follow-up meeting, she would go down the checklist of feedback, item by item, and show how she had incorporated their thoughts into the newest design. Or, if she had decided not to use the feedback, she would share her reasons why. People didn't always agree with Michelle, but they always felt heard. Their input mattered, and they felt like insiders in her process.

Recently, June Cohen said something that really made Michelle's story click. Cohen, the former head of media for TED and current CEO of WaitWhat, explained that in order to chart a truly epic career, "You need to make everyone you enlist a hero, not just in your story, but in their own." In the *Wizard of Oz,* Dorothy enlists the help of the Tin Man, the Scarecrow, and the Lion—by making *them* the hero of their own stories. Cohen says, "If the Scarecrow didn't have a chance of getting a brain, if the Tin Man couldn't get a heart—they wouldn't have braved those attacks from flying monkeys!"[19]

To feel like heroes, we need to know that what we said and what we did made an impact. Penelope Burk is a renowned fundraising researcher who showed the difference it makes when we truly feel that way. More than twenty years ago, Burk noticed that nonprofit leaders were spending the majority of their time and resources recruiting new donors instead of keeping the ones they already had. As a result, nearly 70 percent of an average charity's backers would never give again, and nonprofit leaders would constantly be rebuilding their donor bases from scratch.

"It didn't make any sense," Burk told me. So she decided to study what would happen if a charity spent real time and effort cultivating existing donor relationships. In her experiment, Burk isolated a set of people who had given to a national health charity.

If you were a part of this test group, you received a personal phone call from a member of the board of directors. During this call, you were *not* asked for more money. This was a critical point—the call wasn't being used to sell you again, but rather to express sincere gratitude. You received a heartfelt thank-you for your support, and you learned how your contribution was making a difference. After those phone calls were placed, Burk waited to see which donors stuck around.

What she found was astounding. Two years later, 70 percent of the people who had received the phone call from a board member were still giving to the organization, compared to just 18 percent of those who hadn't. To top it off, donors who remained were now giving 42 percent more than they had at the start.[20]

When Burk shared those results with me, I asked her how one simple phone call could make such a huge difference. She answered my question, in part, by reading a thank-you letter she happened to have sitting on her desk. It was written from one community organizer to another, and the first paragraph began: "We know it's often your role to do the work of making donors and volunteers feel like heroes...and they no doubt are."

Helping people understand their impact isn't a business concept, it's a human concept. We all want to feel as though what we said and what we did mattered. If you're a backer, that can be as simple as knowing your input was heard and utilized—whether that's for a mission, a strategy, or a product.

I got my first glimpse of this in politics. In high school, I knocked on doors for a local politician named John Dingell, and I still remember the annoyed looks on people's faces when I'd ring their doorbell on a Sunday afternoon. By the tail end of the campaign, people's irritation grew because their homes had been visited multiple times by campaign workers who had handed them the *same* piece of literature. "If you give me one more of these pamphlets, I'm voting for the other guy," said one suburban dad.

A decade later, when I was canvassing for another candidate, smartphones had changed everything. Before knocking on a door, I could pull up an app and know the issues that mattered most to that voter because we had taken notes the last time we visited the home. I would say something like "From the last time we chatted, I know you care deeply about K-through-twelve education. Can I give you an update on some of the progress we're making on that front?" As a result, there were fewer door slams and more quality conversations. Voters felt like they were being listened to—that what they said mattered.

We don't typically win people over in one conversation, but through a series of interactions that builds trust and confidence. Even if the last conversation went poorly, you can use the next one to show them how they influenced your work. This type of follow-up is so powerful that it can often change a backer's response from no to yes.

Brian Wood is an innovation strategist at the National Geospatial-Intelligence Agency, which is part of the U.S. Department of Defense. He explained to me, in layman's terms, an internal project he created called Conduit, which used artificial intelligence to help the agency make better decisions more efficiently. But when he pitched decision makers at the Pentagon, they rejected the idea, expressing a laundry list of concerns.

Instead of getting defensive, Wood listened carefully to the feedback. He took detailed notes and created a checklist of things he'd need to address before he returned. Then, weeks later, he scheduled a follow-up meeting.

Just as Michelle the designer had done at a high-tech company, Wood walked Pentagon officials through a modified version of his prototype, showing them exactly how their feedback had been incorporated. When Wood finished his demo, he saw a room full of surprised faces. When he asked if everything was okay, one of the officers cleared his throat and said, "Everything's fine. It's just...no one ever comes back."

Unlike Wood, I never thought to go back to the investors who said no to Rise. That is, until I met an old friend from law school for coffee. Andy patiently listened to me complain about how everyone was passing on my idea. When I was finished, he leaned back in his chair a bit and looked off into the distance for a moment. Then he asked a one-word question: "Why?"

"Why what?" I asked.

"Why did they pass?" he said.

"Because they didn't like the idea," I said, feeling a slight irritation.

"Yes, but why? Why didn't they like the idea?" he pressed.

At that moment, it occurred to me that I hadn't really asked investors who passed *why* they had passed. Typically, I had received a short email saying something like "Sorry. It's just not the right fit for us." But I hadn't followed up and probed further into why.

Later that day, I took Andy's advice and reached out to all the investors who had passed on Rise and asked them what it would have taken for them to say yes. A few of them responded with their version of "Nothing. Just not the right fit for us." But others responded with substantive notes, offering feedback such as "We would have liked to have seen more numbers around retention" or "We'd like to see the engineering team built out a little more so we know you can build a strong consumer product."

Without asking the question, I never would have received the feedback. And now that I had clear direction, I knew to adjust our road map to focus on customer retention and engage a recruiter to help us find engineering talent. About a month later, I emailed those same investors and asked if they'd be willing to take a quick follow-up meeting. I began each of those meetings by restating the concerns they shared and, as soon as that happened, I could feel the room relax. They knew in that moment that I wasn't going to waste their time re-gurgitating the exact same pitch. Then, like Brian Wood inside the Pentagon and Michelle inside her design room, I showed how I had modified our approach using their input and the results we had so far. The new pitch didn't always work, but two venture capitalists who had previously told me no became early investors in Rise.

SHARE JUST ENOUGH

Google used to be the kind of place where you could come up with an idea on a lunch break and have it implemented before you left the office. But within a few short years it outgrew itself multiple times and added layers of bureaucracy. Meeting rooms became packed with opinions. And it began to feel like you couldn't swing a bat without hitting a "decision-maker."

In the midst of this cultural transition, Jake Knapp was pitching a new idea for a video chat interface. As a designer, part of Knapp's job was to rally the growing number of decision-makers around a single creative vision. And, unsurprisingly, these meetings weren't going well.

Knapp discussed the situation with his colleague Serge Lachapelle. Over lunch they reflected on how frictionless and simple these design conversations were when it was just their group. Knapp, who got his degree in visual art, was always sketching on paper or a whiteboard, and everyone seemed to quickly get on the same page.

That's when it struck Lachapelle. Inside their small meetings, Knapp had been using low-fidelity drawings. But for meetings with the higher-ups, he always shared high-fidelity, high-precision mockups. What would happen if they ditched the formal designs and presented these sketches instead?

Knapp decided it was worth a shot. He drew his vision out on a piece of paper, recorded a series of videos of himself walking through his sketches, and shared these with the team. It worked. Knapp was used to receiving criticism but now was receiving suggestions. Looking at the basic sketches, backers were using their imaginations and offering creative input. That feedback gave Knapp the springboard he needed to push the project forward and become a co-founder of Google Meet, which became one of the company's fastest-growing products.

When pitching a new concept, your idea "can't be 100 percent defined," Knapp later told me. That means you need to create room for backers to be a part of it. Share just enough to spark their imagination, but not so much that you give them a reason to say no. Knapp, who's now a bestselling author, stumbled onto a lesson that he's used throughout his career, just like Joel Stein inside the pitch room at CBS.

Another Hollywood writer, Dikran Ornekian, was used to being rejected for all sorts of reasons, but he didn't expect this one. "Madoff?" Ornekian shouted into the phone. What could Bernie Madoff possibly have to do with an action thriller about a colony of werewolves?

Just weeks earlier the industry-trade publication *Variety* had announced that his film, *Lobo,* had been fast-tracked into production. After years of grinding through a day job while writing on nights and weekends, Ornekian finally seemed to be on the path to success. The film was scheduled to shoot in Rio de Janeiro and Ornekian was packing his bags when his manager called to deliver the terrible news. The financiers of the film had lost their money to Madoff's Ponzi scheme. *Lobo*'s green light was now a hard red.

Timing is a big part of being backable, and the timing for Ornekian couldn't have been worse. The Great Recession of 2008 was in full effect, and film financiers were running for the hills. Ornekian sat down with his writing partner, Rylend Grant, at a coffee shop in Santa Monica. It took all their strength not to meet at a bar instead. With *Lobo* collecting dust on a shelf, they needed another idea that would make them money—and time was of the essence. The economy might have been in a slump, but the rent wasn't getting any cheaper in Southern California.

At the top of their list was an idea they had been talking about off and on for years. A master thief reluctantly agrees to teach a group of rough-and-tumble kids the true craft of taking down a score. It was part heist movie, part *Karate Kid*. They called it *Thief Coach*.

As excited as they were about the idea, they wondered whether they should even give *Thief Coach* a try. Hollywood studios were already turning away from original screenplays and toward established intellectual property. Worse, it would take Ornekian and Grant six months to write a new screenplay—and they simply couldn't afford (financially and mentally) to invest that time again with zero return.

During this period, the duo landed a meeting with Derek Haas, one of the top screenwriters in town and creator of the hit TV show *Chicago Fire*. He also ran a website, Popcorn Fiction, that was publishing short stories by screenwriters, mostly big-time screenwriters, but he liked the pitch for *Thief Coach* and encouraged them to try writing it as a short story instead.

It sounded like the perfect way to give the idea a test run. They could knock out a 30-page short-story version of *Thief Coach* a lot quicker than they could a 120-page screenplay. And while there was still no promise of a financial return, at least it would be published—at least it would exist in the real world, unlike *Lobo* and so many other unmade scripts.

Not long after "Thief Coach" was published on Popcorn Fiction, with little noise or fanfare, Ornekian was about to take his usual jog by the Pacific Ocean when he noticed a voicemail from his manager. There was a time when he would have checked it immediately, but after years of bad news, he decided it could wait until after his run. When Ornekian finally listened, it was garbled and nonsensical. All he could make out was "Justin loves it!"

While the public reaction to "Thief Coach" was relatively muted, the short story had been quietly circulating from desk to desk of influential producers and directors until it finally made its way to Justin Lin, director of several *Fast and Furious* movies. Lin loved the story so much that he immediately called a meeting.

But in this meeting, Ornekian and Grant didn't end up pitching Lin as much as Lin ended up pitching them. When Lin read "Thief Coach," it sparked his own ideas for how the full-length story could unfold. And because the story was still high-level, without the details of a fully baked screenplay, the door was open for real collaboration, and that excited Lin. After years of struggling to get inside rooms like this, Ornekian and Grant flipped one of Hollywood's hottest directors into an insider.

STEP 6:

PLAY EXHIBITION MATCHES

When Oren Jacob was an intern at a computer graphics startup called Pixar, Steve Jobs, the CEO, decided the company would change direction from hardware and software to animation and laid off more than half the employees. Everyone was laid off in an instant, and Jacob assumed that he was as well. Over the weekend, Jacob was trying to figure out what to do next. That's when his dad asked him, "What would happen if you just went back on Monday as if nothing has changed?" Jacob figured he had nothing to lose, so he gave it a shot.

On Monday morning, he showed up to the weekly all-hands meeting, which had been reduced to fewer than fifty people. The layoffs had happened so swiftly that everyone was scanning the room to figure out who had made it through. Jacob got a couple of blank stares and even a raised eyebrow or two, but no one asked the obvious question: "Why did they keep the intern?"

After the meeting, Jacob tried to make himself look busy by seeking out a task—anything to be productive. He did it the next day and the next after that. It was the beginning of what turned into a twenty-year career where he climbed from intern to technical director of *A Bug's Life* to supervising technical director of *Finding Nemo* and finally chief technology officer for all of Pixar.

Those two decades put Jacob in the nexus of the backable universe. From *Toy Story* to *Brave*, Jacob played a key role in pivoting Pixar from a graphics company to Hollywood's premier animation studio. Along the way, he heard thousands of pitches from every corner of the company—from screenplays to technical proposals to business plans. He personally pitched ideas to Steve Jobs and to Ed Catmull, the co-founder of Pixar. So you can imagine how excited I was to sit down with Jacob to understand what he'd learned about being backable behind the Willy Wonka walls of Pixar.

At first, his answer felt disappointing. After twenty years at the studio, Jacob says your likelihood of success inside a pitch room depends on one key thing: *practice*. Whether you're interviewing for a job, sharing a new idea with your team, or raising money from an investor, "a pitch is a live performance." Not practicing beforehand is like an actor not rehearsing before the main show.

I felt Jacob was oversimplifying, so I challenged him to walk me through a real-life scenario—an interview I had completely blown with Jack Dorsey some years prior. You might remember this story from the introduction, but let me share a few additional, even more embarrassing, details. Dorsey, the co-founder of Twitter, had just started his newest company, Square, where I was interviewing for a product management role. In the first two minutes of my interview with Dorsey, he threw me a softball: "How do you think about product development?"

Now, just so you have context, I had spent the past few years living and breathing product development. I had managed product development teams, written product development papers, and spoken at product development conferences. But somehow when Dorsey asked me simply how "I think" about product development, my answer came out in a jumbled mess.

I remember wrapping up my answer like a nervous spelling bee contestant, and seeing Dorsey's demeanor fade from full attention to full-on confusion. Shortly after, he politely excused himself. Needless to say, I didn't get the job.

Recapping the story, I recoiled inside, but Jacob found it entertaining. After a few laughs, he asked me a simple question: "Did you practice before that interview?" Yes, I responded. I did my research, wrote down notes, and prepped questions—all the things we do to prepare for an interview.

"But did you practice?" Jacob asked again.

"You mean did I actually *rehearse* what I was going to say? No."

Jacob gave me a look—not all that different from the one Jack Dorsey had given me. He asked, "When you were studying for a test in law school, would you take practice tests?" I nodded—without those practice exams, I wouldn't have gotten through law school. Jacob leaned in. "So, for a law school exam you would spend hours practicing, but for a meeting that could have changed your career, you didn't practice at all?"

He wasn't trying to make me feel bad, but Jacob's words landed like a punch to the gut. And not just because of the Jack Dorsey meeting. I began to reflect on every meaningful interaction in my career. All the presentations, interviews, coffees—really any situation where I had an opportunity to shine. I couldn't think of a time when I actually practiced before the meeting.

Having now coached founders and creators, I've seen first-hand how exceedingly rare it is for someone to practice before their pitch. We'll spend hours researching, outlining, pulling together slides—but very little time practicing what we're going to share. The feeling seems to be that if we have the right content and we know it well enough, then there's no need for practice.

But I've found that backable people tend to practice their pitch extensively before walking into the room. They practice with friends, family, and colleagues. They're rehearsing on jogs with running partners, in the break room, and during happy hour. They prepare themselves for high-stakes pitches through lots of low-stakes practice sessions—what I now call exhibition matches.

NO VENUE IS TOO SMALL

Years ago, I got a call from my friend Lance, who was both giddy and intoxicated. After some struggle, he was able to co-herently explain what had just happened. On a midweek night, Lance and another friend stumbled into the Comedy Cellar, a tiny underground comedy venue in New York City. The place was half-empty and Lance was admitted for a mere $5. He sat at a table in the front row and watched performances from comedians he'd never heard of. Close to last call, as he was getting ready to leave, a surprised-looking MC got up on stage. "Ladies and gentlemen...you'll never guess who's here," he said and gave a slightly longer than usual pause. "Help me welcome...Jerry Seinfeld!"

This was only months after the series finale of his show, and Jerry Seinfeld was the most in-demand comedian on the planet, easily selling out venues like Madison Square Garden. But there was Lance with a $5 ticket stub buried in his right pocket, listening to a comedy legend.

When Jerry Seinfeld's show went off the air, he did something that most fans didn't expect—he went back to performing at the tiny clubs that gave him his start twenty years prior. Why? Because Seinfeld wanted to practice new material inside low-stakes venues before going back to performing in front of sold-out stadiums.

For backable people, no venue is too small for an exhibition match. The only requirement is the ability to practice in front of someone other than yourself. Simply having a real human staring at you is enough to put you into real practice mode. I've now played plenty of exhibition matches in front of my eight-year-old daughter.

The key is to treat each one of these exhibition matches as if you were in front of a real backer. I used to make the mistake of giving a director's commentary during my exhibition matches. I'd say things like, "First I'm going to talk about the size of the digital therapeutics market; then I'll discuss how we're different from the competitors." But that's not a real exhibition match. When Seinfeld performed in front of audiences at half-filled places like the Comedy Cellar, he still treated it like a sold-out stadium and performed his actual set.

Hunter Walk invests in companies at their earliest stage and then works with those founders to help them raise additional funding. While they're practicing together, founders will sometimes try to shift to voice-over mode, where they're no longer giving the pitch, but rather giving a description of the pitch. If a founder starts saying something like "And this slide is where

I'll show the investor our Go to Market strategy," Walk will say, "Stop. We're going to do this in real time."[1]

Oren Jacob from Pixar considers this an essential rule. "When you're practicing, don't share an overview of what you're going to share. Share *exactly* what you're going to share." Not only is that better for your practice; it's better for the audience. Jacob told me about the time his colleague Andrew Stanton pitched *Finding Nemo* to the key marketing partners for the film. These were the merchandising executives who decided how much to invest in creating everything from toys to toddler toilet lids. Because it's such an important presentation, a team of people will typically take the stage, armed with lots of visuals. Not Stanton. He walked onstage alone, without any visuals in hand, and for the next ninety minutes delivered what Jacob described as a "world-class, Olympic-caliber pitch."

How? By taking the executives right into the story—as if they were watching the film. It wasn't a preview or a description; it was an actual one-man show of *Finding Nemo*. When it came time to introduce the seagull characters in the film, Stanton didn't say, "The seagulls are funny because they compete with each other for food, shouting 'mine' at each other." Instead, Stanton tilted his head up like a seagull and shouted, "Mine! Mine! Mine!" to a highly entertained group of advertising executives. Again, they weren't getting a preview of the story. They were getting the actual story. Stanton's one-man performance helped lead to one of the larger merchandising buys of all time.

When a friend asks what you're working on, instead of giving them the thirty-second summary, ask, "Do you have fifteen minutes for me to practice my pitch?" I've found that playing exhibition matches not only deepens my practice but deepens my relationships. Friends and family may like to be invited into your creative process. And if no venue is too small, the world becomes your stadium.

BE WILLING TO BE EMBARRASSED

The first practice session is always the hardest, because you're letting someone else see the roughest edges of your pitch. One of the big reasons I never played exhibition matches is because I wanted to avoid any negative feedback.

But Reid Hoffman showed me how this line of thinking was holding me back. One of the first projects I worked on as an employee at Mozilla was a product called Themes, which let you customize the look and feel of your Firefox internet browser. A few months into the project, Hoffman, who was on Mozilla's board, asked me how customers were responding to the product. I answered that we hadn't tested yet with customers because the product wasn't ready. He looked at me and said, "If you're not embarrassed by the first version of your product, then you've launched too late."

Backable people have taught me that long-term success can come from short-term embarrassment. Compelling presenters who seem to speak naturally and off the cuff are often the product of lots of practice rounds. They've practiced so much that their speech seems unpracticed. Maureen Taylor runs a communication coaching service in Silicon Valley that works with senior leaders inside companies like Disney, General Electric, and Hilton. When I asked her how many of her clients were naturals, she didn't hesitate before saying, "None of them."

Eric Schmidt, the former CEO of Google, is a remarkable

example. Schmidt is regarded as one of the more articulate people in Silicon Valley, but earlier in his career at Sun Micro-systems, he was viewed as quiet and contemplative—the kind of guy who rarely raised his ideas in a meeting. Taylor told me that Schmidt decided to take action and become a "student of communication." He learned how to fully express his ideas during his time at Sun, which led him to larger roles inside the company and eventually put him on the radar of Google's co-founders, Larry Page and Sergey Brin.

Again, it's easy to assume that compelling communicators are naturals; but more often than not, they're the product of deliberate practice and personal reinvention. To get to where they are, they played lots of exhibition matches.

DON'T ASK, "WHAT DO YOU THINK?"

After explaining an idea to a friend, I'll often ask them to explain it back to me. Not only does that help me understand whether the idea is landing, but it also helps me pick up new ways to explain it. When I first thought about writing this book, the bestselling author Dan Pink listened to my pitch and then explained it back to me, only far more eloquently. "The most exceptional people aren't just brilliant...they're backable," he said. If you remember a similar line from the introduction of this book, that was his.

Asking people to repeat my idea back to me always gives me a sense of what's actually resonating. It helps me prune away the parts that aren't working and dial up the dialogue that is. This is similar to how the film industry uses "table reads," where actors and actresses sit around a table to read a full screenplay aloud. The director will tune in to how the room is reacting to the lines. Those that fall flat might get cut, while others get amped up.

Hunter Walk, the investor we met a few pages ago, told me he brings the same approach to helping startups raise funding. He and a founder will print out the pitch deck and put an asterisk on slides that, on a scale of one to ten, "should be dialed up to an eleven."

The goal of an exhibition match is to get the most direct feedback possible. After giving a practice pitch, don't ask the question "What do you think?" It almost never leads to the type of insight you need to get prepared for a difficult backer. Instead, dig beneath surface-level feedback by asking more specific questions.

Dr. Tom Lee is the founder of One Medical, which is one of the fastest-growing primary care providers in the world. It's also the company that acquired Rise. Today One Medical is publicly traded and serves nearly five hundred thousand patients,[2] but it started as a one-man operation. Early patients were surprised when they walked in to see Lee answering phone calls, taking vitals, and administering flu shots.

During his training, Lee discovered how the right questions could uncover root issues. Lee says that if a patient came in with a headache, for example, he learned to ask not "Why did you decide to come in?" but rather "Why did you decide to come in *today*?" That one additional word helped get to the source of the problem, which Lee says was often tied to the stress of a job or family situation.

He began to see questions as medical instruments—the wrong instruments led to useless answers. When he started One Medical, most medical providers would ask their patients, "How satisfied were you with your visit?" But Lee felt like that question was a blunt instrument that didn't probe deep enough. "Almost everyone circled four out of five."

Lee decided to ask each patient a much more specific question. "On a scale of one to ten, how likely would you be to recommend me to a friend?" Then he'd dig into why each patient scored the way they did, so he could apply what he learned to his next patient's experience. Lee says that question, known by marketers as a Net Promoter Score, was a much more sensitive instrument that allowed him to "pick up a lot more defects."

By not settling for the standard patient satisfaction question, Lee was able to get past the obvious and design what a *Business Insider* reporter called "the best medical practice I've ever used"[3] and what *Fast Company* named the number one most innovative company in health (Apple was number two).[4]

Lee showed me what's possible when we go beyond softball questions like "What do you think?" As much as we may enjoy hearing "I like it," this kind of feedback won't get us very far. The most backable people know this. That's why every night after filming *The Daily Show,* instead of going straight home to his family, Jon Stewart would huddle with the show's producers in a windowless room with a few chairs for a post-mortem. Snacking on his nightly post-show bowl of cut fruit, Stewart would ask "what went right" but mainly probed into "what we could have done better."

Steve Bodow, the show's head writer and executive producer, was in the room for nearly two thousand postmortems. He recalls how one night they questioned why one of the show's montage reels had received a flat reaction from the audience. By digging beneath the obvious answers, they discovered that writers had submitted the clips without timestamps, which then required the video team to spend twenty extra minutes searching the footage. "Sounds like a small thing," says Bodow. "But because they didn't have enough time to refine the video editing, the joke wasn't set up properly—and that's why it tanked."

One final point about gathering the right feedback: sometimes the best insight comes from how people act, not what they say. A friend may not want to hurt your feelings, so pay attention to nonverbal cues—facial expressions, nodding, smiling at the right moments—to tell whether your delivery is landing.

When testing new product concepts with customers, some top researchers skip verbal feedback altogether and pay attention to just the nonverbal behavior. When I was at Groupon, my team and I stopped asking beta customers what they thought of a new design and simply watched the way they interacted with it. We got much more accurate feedback that way. Sometimes customers would say they preferred one design but then spend a lot more time interacting with the alternative.

Author Neil Strauss told me that when he's done writing a book, he prints it out and reads the entire manuscript aloud to someone he trusts. But he almost never asks for their feedback. Instead, during his read-through, he'll pay close attention to their facial expressions and make little notes to himself in the margins based on their reactions. Strauss considers this practice one of his secrets to success, in his case seven *New York Times* bestsellers.

BUILD YOUR BACKABLE CIRCLE

Esther Perel is a psychotherapist and an expert on relationships and sexuality. Perel argues that marriages fail because we expect our partner to give us "what once an entire village used to provide." Perel says we put it on one person to "give me belonging, give me identity, give me continuity, but give me transcendence and mystery and awe all in one. Give me comfort, give me edge. Give me novelty, give me familiarity. Give me predictability, give me surprise." And when they fall short on delivering on all of this, we blame them.[5]

Marriage counselors often challenge their clients to shift this burden from one person to a circle of people, including friends and family, each of whom fills a different need. Your spouse or partner is part of the circle, but not the full circle required to make you feel whole.

Strange as it may sound, this is also sage professional advice. Peter Thiel, the co-founder of PayPal and Palantir—and backer of startups including Yelp, Facebook, and Spotify—emphasizes the importance of his circle. He says the one thing he tries to do every day is to have a conversation with "some of the smartest people I know and continue to develop my thinking."[6]

Backable people like Thiel tend to build a circle of trusted advisers who bring different personalities and points of view. You'll end up playing most of your exhibition matches with the individuals in this circle. They will wind up being a vital part of your backable journey. And while each "backable circle" is different, there are four specific types of people (the four Cs) I like to have in mine.

The first is your collaborator. This is someone who's going to help you expand your idea and improve your delivery. They're not going to agree with everything you say, but all feedback is going to feel productive. When you're with a collaborator, you feel like you're in a musical jam session—riffing off each other and lifting your concept to a better place.

Law school students have a reputation for being more competitive than collaborative, but the exception at Northwestern was Evan Eschmeyer, a former NBA player who had gone back to school after blowing out his knee. While most classes were filled with debate and dissent, he would always be the one bridging together arguments. As Eschmeyer and I became friends, I began to understand just how deep his collaborative spirit ran.

In 2001, the Dallas Mavericks were championship contenders, and commentators were surprised when owner Mark Cuban recruited Eschmeyer to the team. He was relatively unknown, yet Cuban wasn't paying attention to star status. Instead he was focused on a metric called plus-minus. Rather than measuring how well you play on the court, plus-minus measures how well *your teammates* perform when you're on the court. While Eschmeyer's individual statistics were barely average, his plus-minus was one of the best in the entire league. When he was in the game, his teammates excelled.

Eschmeyer carried his plus-minus attitude off the court, through law school, and into the professional world. Today he's seen as a trusted adviser to CEOs and has been one of my closest collaborators. When Rise was still in the idea phase, he was one of my first calls. When I started to think about writing this book, he was one of my first calls. In both cases, he listened intently and took notes. Then we did a jam session on how to make it better.

The second type of person I recommend for the early days of a new idea is your coach. While your collaborator will help you figure out if your idea is right for the world, your coach will also help you understand if an idea is right for *you*. As we discussed in Step 1, just because an idea is a good fit for the market doesn't mean it's a good fit for you. My wife, Leena, is my coach. I'm constantly bringing ideas to her—sometimes annoyingly so. As a journalist who's written for *Fortune* magazine, Leena has a strong sense of whether something fits the market, but she has an even stronger sense of whether an idea fits me. The filter she uses isn't simply "Is this a good idea?" but rather "Is this a good idea for Suneel?"

A few weeks ago I told her my idea for an "Emotional Rotten Tomatoes," which would show how a movie was likely to make you feel. After giving it some thought she came back with "Sounds like it could work, but it doesn't feel like something you'd really want to build." And she was right, because a couple of weeks later I had all but forgotten about the idea (though I still think it could work).

The third C is your cheerleader. This isn't the person who's going to give you critical feedback, but rather the person who's going to make you feel confident before you get in the room. Hockey players will warm their goalie up before a game with practice shots that are easy to block. The goal, in those final minutes, is to build the goalie's assurance, not his skill.

Your cheerleader can be anyone—a friend, a co-worker, a spouse, or a parent. *Fast Company* magazine named Ellen Levy the "most connected woman in Silicon Valley." Her network ranges from members of Congress to CEOs of publicly traded companies. Yet when I asked her who she goes to for confidence before an important pitch, she smiled and said, "That one's easy. It's my mom."

I've come to see the fourth C—your "Cheddar"—as the most pivotal role in your circle. Your Cheddar is the person who will deliberately poke holes in your ideas, sometimes in a way that is deeply unsettling.

As a Detroiter, I loved *8 Mile* and named Cheddar after one of Eminem's friends in the film. Throughout the movie, Eminem's friends are constantly building him up, except for Cheddar. In the last scene, Eminem's crew is getting him ready for his final rap battle, giving him positive encouragement, when Cheddar all of a sudden says something to the tune of "What if he brings up the fact that your girlfriend just cheated on you?"

While everyone dismisses Cheddar immediately, Eminem takes a moment and realizes it's a valid point. So when Eminem takes the stage, he brings up the girlfriend situation first (steering into the objection), taking the wind out of his opponent's sails. This is what a good Cheddar does. They ask the tough questions so that we're not hearing them for the first time from a backer.

Most of us tend to steer clear of the Cheddars in our life. We run away from people who can be the most critical of our ideas. But these are the people who get us best prepared, because backers are a lot like Cheddar. Their job is to find your blind spots. By playing exhibition matches with their Cheddars, backable people discover the hidden problems with their own ideas. And as investor Charlie Munger says, "knowing what you don't know is more useful than being brilliant."[7]

When I was struggling to get investors interested in Rise, I was introduced to Leah Solivan, the founder and then CEO of TaskRabbit, one of the hotter online marketplaces at the time. We met at Solivan's go-to breakfast spot in San Mateo for our exhibition match and I pitched her as if she were an investor. When I finished, her nonverbals told me everything—she didn't just have simple modifications in mind, my pitch needed an overhaul. We went through her list—my presentation was too long; it was bloated with facts and figures; it was missing a concise, memorable story. Solivan poked holes but then helped me rebuild a new outline from scratch. After Solivan left the diner to go on with her day, I stayed. Sitting alone at that counter, I ordered another cup of coffee and got to work.

THE RULE OF 21

In February of 1960, Ella Fitzgerald sang "Mack the Knife" to a large crowd in West Berlin. The song was popularized by artists like Bobby Darin, Louis Armstrong, and Frank Sinatra, but this was the first time the crowd had heard a woman sing it. It was a special moment in musical history that was almost ruined when halfway through Fitzgerald forgot the lyrics.

But instead of stopping, Fitzgerald kept singing, playfully, joyfully inventing new lyrics as she went. The crowd roared in appreciation, and the recording earned her Best Female Vocal Performance at the Third Annual Grammy Awards in 1961.

Meetings can easily take a turn like Fitzgerald's performance. You get asked an unexpected question; the connection to your laptop stops working; people shuffle in and out of the room. Some people are natural improvisers, and can easily flow through stumbles and interruptions. But more often than not, people who have reached this level of fluidity have built what I refer to as "recovery muscle." They're so comfortable with their material that they welcome curveball moments.

Josh Linkner is an award-winning jazz musician and keynote speaker. Linkner will be the first to tell you that the great musicians and speakers are able to pull off "Mack the Knife" performances like Fitzgerald's, not from believing that everything will go right—but from being confident enough for everything to go wrong.

Here's how Linkner described that feeling of confidence to

me: "When I play jazz, I go into a gig with a lot of confidence. But the confidence isn't what you think. It's not that I'm going to play it perfectly. It's knowing that I'm *for sure* going to screw something up. But because I've practiced so much, I have confidence that I can recover. Knowing that makes me feel bulletproof onstage."

I, too, wanted to feel bulletproof onstage. As I was preparing to give a speech to more than seven hundred fund managers in California, I asked Linkner how many reps—how many exhibition matches—I needed to play. His answer made my face fall. "Twenty-one practice rounds," Linkner said. Up to that point, I couldn't remember practicing anything twenty-one times. And yet, when I later shared the Rule of 21 with highly backable people, no one batted an eye.

So, I got started. I did my first few exhibition matches with my wife and kids, until they got tired of hearing my speech. Then I went to friends. Calling someone I hadn't spoken to in a while and asking, "Would you mind if I gave you a practice run of my speech over Zoom?" felt awkward. But very few people declined and I found myself not only reconnecting with friends, but also inching closer to my target of twenty-one.

Around my tenth practice round, I felt something new. I knew the material so well that I no longer needed to focus on it. Instead, I could use that attention span to survey my audience. I could observe how each message was landing, and make adjustments along the way. In earlier practice rounds, if someone seemed confused, I'd simply move on to the next point. Now I found myself being able to adjust on the fly—I would slow down and re-emphasize for clarity. If they seemed excited, I'd dial up my energy even more. If they laughed, I'd smile with them. My talk was starting to feel more like a dance than a pitch.

Around my fifteenth exhibition match, I felt unflappable. My three-year-old daughter could kick open the door in the middle of a practice session and drag me to the kitchen to pour her a glass of milk, and I could still pick up where I left off without losing any momentum. I began to understand why this Ella Fitzgerald level of mastery matters in the pitch room. Backers will rarely sit quietly through an entire pitch, unless they're bored. They cut in with questions, ask you to go back, ask you to jump ahead. None of this is bad, because it means your backer is actually engaged. And if you can glide through the choppiness—jumping from point 3 to point 9 and then transitioning smoothly back to 4—those are the moments when your confidence shines through.

By the time I was backstage for my speech, I had practiced twenty-one times and was almost hoping for a mishap so that I could flex my newly built recovery muscles. I finally understood what it was like to feel bulletproof.

REBOOT YOUR STYLE

If you play enough exhibition matches, you'll start to see patterns in the feedback. Sometimes you'll come to the realization that your entire pitch isn't working. Instead of throwing away your dream, have the courage to reboot your style and begin again. Nearly every successful person has done this. Want proof? Search for an old speech of someone you admire and notice how their communication style has changed.

On July 27, 2004, I was working as a junior-level writer at the Democratic National Convention. It was a Tuesday, the second of three nights in Boston packed with speeches from every household name in the Democratic Party. My job was to help make sure each speaker—from Hillary Clinton to the Reverend Al Sharpton—had what they needed before they went onstage.

But in a sea of political heavyweights, there was one speaker I had never seen before. As he scribbled on a yellow notepad in the corner of our makeshift working room, I quietly asked one of the other backstage managers who he was. The manager couldn't remember his name, just that he was "a state senator from Illinois."

That "state senator" happened to be Barack Obama, and when he took the stage that night, I got a backstage view of his coming-out party. While the world was watching Obama, I felt like I was watching the world. I saw a tidal wave of energy rip through the crowd, electrifying everyone it touched. I saw parents lifting children to their shoulders, hardened politicos wiping back tears, and camera operators sidestepping their tripods to watch with human eyes. Before that speech, most people in the stadium didn't know Obama's name. Hours after the convention finished for the night, I watched as people stayed behind to scrounge for Obama paraphernalia on the stadium floor.

We know how the story unfolded from there, but it's worth taking a moment to revisit how it began. Four years before that speech, Barack Obama ran for Congress and was defeated by a two-to-one margin. After the loss, the Obama family was $60,000 in debt, Michelle wasn't happy, and Barack was considering giving up his political aspirations altogether.

And things were about to get worse. After losing his election, Obama decided to fly out for the 2000 Democratic National Convention, which was being held in Los Angeles. After landing at LAX, he tried to rent a car, but his credit card was declined. Then, after finding a way to the convention, he was denied admission into the main auditorium. When Al Gore accepted his nomination that night, Barack Obama was standing outside the convention, watching on a monitor.[8] Four years later, he would be the keynote speaker.

What happened in those four years? Obama began again. He hit the reset button and started from scratch. It's hard to believe now, but back then Barack Obama was seen as boring. Reporters described him as "stilted" and "professorial." His stump speech felt like a lecture. Ted McClelland, a journalist who covered Obama during his congressional loss, said that his speeches were so dry they "sucked the life out of the room."[9]

That all changed when he rebooted his style, thanks in part to a new ally—the Reverend Jesse Jackson. While Obama knew how to educate an audience, the reverend knew how to move an audience. If he was going to reach the highest levels of office, Obama needed both. So Jackson helped Obama become a frequent speaker for his coalition, the Rainbow PUSH. It was there that Obama played many exhibition matches, honing a style that would ultimately become the foundation for his 2004 keynote.[10]

Looking back on that period, Obama says that it was losing an election that showed him how to win. "It taught me the importance of campaigning not based on a bunch of whitepapers and policy prescriptions but telling a story," he said.[11] That wisdom helped rebrand Obama from neighborhood politician to a national leader. But none of that would have happened had he not been willing to reinvent his own style.

STEP 7:

LET GO OF YOUR EGO

In 1959, a young biologist named Dr. George Schaller went to Central Africa to study mountain gorillas. At the time, the perception was that these were vicious, dangerous beasts. Something to fear. But after living among them for two years, Schaller discovered that gorillas were in fact gentle, compassionate, and extremely intelligent, with complex social structures. When he returned to present his groundbreaking findings, a biologist in the audience asked, "Dr. Schaller, we've been studying these creatures for centuries and we didn't know any of this. How did you get such detailed information?"

"It's simple," Schaller replied. "I didn't carry a gun."[1]

While it was common practice for researchers to stash a weapon in their backpacks in case something went wrong, Schaller never did. He believed you could hide a gun, but you could never hide your *attitude* when you carried a gun. No smile or gentleness could fully cover your unease, and the gorillas could always pick up on that.

After many years of struggling to become backable, I came to realize that the gun inside my backpack was my ego. That my extreme desire to impress people in the room had created distance, not connection. No matter how professional or friendly I acted, people could always tell when I wasn't at ease.

The other techniques in this book got me comfortable with content, but I still had to learn to get truly comfortable with myself. I had to learn to let go of my ego—to express, rather than impress.

SHOW, DON'T TELL

A few months ago, inside the office of a venture capital firm, I met an extremely likable startup founder from New York who was pitching a new pizza-delivery app. As a customer, you could tap one button and get your favorite type of pizza delivered. The founder came from five generations of pizzeria owners. As he and I spoke in the conference room while waiting for the other investors to arrive, he showed me a photo of his great-great-grandfather, who had opened the family's first pizzeria in a small town in Italy. I was immediately charmed by this guy. He had a thick Brooklyn accent, a genuine smile, and a sense of ease.

But as more investors started filtering in, I saw his demeanor shift. He pulled back his smile and pushed forward a more serious, solemn attitude. When he began going through his slide deck, his easy style seemed to evaporate. The content was interesting (and also reminded me why a third of Americans are obese). Three billion pizzas are sold every year. Each man, woman, and child eats an average of twenty-three pounds of pizza annually.[2] From 2010 to 2017, there was only one company that outperformed Netflix, Apple, and Google on the public market: Domino's Pizza.[3] And though the slides were well designed and the content was strong, his delivery fell flat. Looking around the table, I could see the boredom building. The investors in the room were beginning to check their phones. I knew, from personal experience, that he was losing them. And once you lose your audience, it's very hard to get them back.

Then I remembered how proud he was to show me his great-great-grandfather. If only I could shift him back to show mode. So I blurted out, "Do you have the app on your phone?" Seeing the confused looks around the table, the founder said, "Yeah. I do. Want to take a look?" I said yes and walked right up, leaning over his shoulder. One by one, the other investors slowly rose from their seats.

That's when the switch flipped. With all of us huddled around the founder's iPhone, his energy replenished. His personality shifted back to how it was when he shared with me his family story. As he swiped to unveil the different features in the app, I saw the investors put away their phones and begin to ask questions. He had their interest, and a few weeks later, he got their investment.

I find that in every pitch, no matter the industry or setting, people are more confident when they're in "huddle mode," showing their idea rather than describing it. Less than six months into his legal career, Jordan Roberts found himself presenting to an audience of hard-hitting lawyers who were negotiating Facebook's offer to buy WhatsApp for nearly $20 billion, their largest acquisition by far. These types of deals typically take months to negotiate, but Mark Zuckerberg gave his team four days. It was a Sunday morning and the people inside the conference room had been working around the clock. They were sleep deprived and tired of take-out food.[4]

Now a first-year attorney was about to walk them through some of the most important numbers of the deal. Years later, I asked Roberts, "Were you nervous? Did you have doubts?" Yes and yes. But Roberts performed so well inside that room that he earned the immediate respect of highly established dealmakers, and a position on the *Forbes* 30 Under 30 list. How did he deliver such a stellar presentation?

By not delivering a presentation at all. Instead of using slides, Roberts simply projected his spreadsheet and walked the attorneys in the room through his numbers. "I wasn't presenting," he told me. "I was just showing them the way I thought about it."

FORGET YOURSELF

When you walk into a room to present your idea, the spotlight is on you. Your job is to turn that spotlight away from you and toward your message.

Years into building Rise, we needed a few key partnerships to help grow our customer base and generate more revenue, which in turn could help us raise more funding. I began to pitch large companies like Aetna, Weight Watchers, and Fitbit—companies that seemed like a logical, even obvious fit. And yet, every one of them passed.

Around this time, communications guru Maureen Taylor, whom we met earlier in the book, quoted Charlie Parker: "You've got to learn your instrument. Then you practice, practice, practice. And then, when you finally get up there on the bandstand, forget all that and just wail." Riffing off of Parker, Taylor shared two words that have become my mantra: "Forget yourself."

I take those two words with me everywhere—to meetings, to presentations, even to dinners with friends. Those two words helped Rise land successful partnerships, and our next rounds of funding.

And I've seen those two words work magic for others. Take Liz, a marketing leader who had spent the past fifteen years managing large teams inside high-growth companies. Liz was raised in Tel Aviv and served in the Israeli army before immigrating to the United States. During our one-on-one meetings, she spoke assertively, with a sort of innate ease that I could only dream of. She immediately came across as backable. Why would someone like her need my help?

It turns out that Liz was extremely confident outside the boardroom. But when in front of a group, and particularly when sharing a new idea, she would sweat through her clothes. "My voice shrinks. My confidence shrinks. I shrink."

When Liz was presenting, she felt the spotlight burning brightly on her, and our job was to turn it away from her—and toward her ideas. A senior talent agent at the Creative Artists Agency once told me that we tend to speak more confidently when we're representing someone else. "That's why," he said, "I'm always better at selling a client than I am at selling myself." It can also explain why some of his clients who are quiet offscreen become powerhouses when they're playing a character. James Earl Jones and Marilyn Monroe, who both struggled with stuttering, spoke impeccably when the cameras rolled.[5] I wondered whether we could bring that same mindset to Liz inside the boardroom. What if she wasn't representing herself to the board, but rather her customer?

When I shared the concept with Liz, it clicked immediately. "I could be like an agent for my customer instead of some VP of marketing," she said. Days later, she entered the meeting with the "agent" mindset. When a board member pressed her during Q&A on the new analytics tool, she walked him through what her customer's life is like without the tool. "Here's what her workflow looks like now," she began.

The board green-lighted Liz's new idea. After the meeting, the CEO of the company pulled her aside to let her know it was one of the more effective marketing presentations she had ever seen. Today, Liz is a sought-after speaker for large companies and marketing associations. And her approach is always the same—turn the spotlight away from her and toward her ideas.

Liz and I may have stumbled onto the idea of acting like an agent, but it turns out to be part of a backability pattern. We tend to be more passionate when we're advocating for someone or something other than ourselves.

Gregg Spiridellis is the co-creator of JibJab, a digital entertainment studio made famous for its "This Land" video during the 2004 presidential election. Before Spiridellis enters the pitch room he'll read emails like the one from a son who used JibJab to help his family laugh during his father's battle with cancer. When staffers at Kiva, a nonprofit that lends money to entrepreneurs across the globe, were trying to secure funding from new donors, they would watch videos from the people they helped finance before entering the room. These weren't necessarily stories they shared during the pitch. The purpose was to remind themselves whom they were serving so they could forget themselves inside the room.

Leah Solivan, the founder we met earlier, was rejected multiple times before raising funding for TaskRabbit. She remained confident inside the pitch room by focusing on what her customer needed. "I just believed this idea could help people," she told me. This was almost the exact answer

I received when talking to Roberta Baskin, an investigative journalist whose reporting has cleaned up child labor practices, reshaped industries, and saved lives.

It all started when Baskin saw Beech-Nut, a baby food company, distributing flyers to new mothers claiming that homemade baby food was dangerous for infants.[6] At the time Baskin was working for the Consumer Affairs office of Syracuse, New York, and demanded that Beech-Nut send a more truthful follow-up message. When they ignored her, she brainstormed the most effective ways she could get the message directly to the people. She applied for a job at a local television station.

The problem was that she didn't have any experience as a reporter, or a degree in journalism. In fact, she didn't even have a college degree. When, through sheer persistence, Baskin managed to get an audition, it did not go well. She convinced them to give her another shot. They did, and again, she was rejected.

Most people would have given up at this point. But Baskin called the news director and said, "Hire me at the lowest salary you can pay and don't put me on the air until you think I'm ready." By relenting, he kickstarted one of the more influential careers in investigative journalism. Baskin went on to stop a pediatric dental chain from performing unnecessary root canals on babies as part of an insurance scam and help get cancer-causing agents removed from beer.

She's led major investigations for ABC's *20/20* and the *CBS Evening News,* winning countless awards in the process. Yet when I asked Baskin to reflect on her career and the persistence it took to get that first job, I got a genuine sense that it was never really about her. "People needed to know about Beech-Nut."

FIND THE PASSIONATE FEW

Trevor McFedries was using a standard template he'd found on how to pitch a venture capitalist. It wasn't working. He was looking for investment into an AI-generated avatar, "Lil Miquela," who displayed more humanity on Instagram than most people. But he'd been rejected more than thirty times. And after sinking more than $50,000 into the project, he was running out of money and on the brink of calling it quits.

Then McFedries remembered something he had learned years earlier, when he was a DJ in the hip-hop music scene. McFedries, also known as Yung Skeeter and DJ Skeet Skeet, could be found spinning at small venues outside Manhattan, looking out at a crowd of club-goers wearing Yankees caps. He didn't need a crystal ball to know what kind of music they craved. He'd fire up the first Jay-Z tune of the night, and the crowd would flood the dance floor. One after another, he rotated through hip-hop tracks that got him approving looks, hands in the air, and praise from the manager.

All the while McFedries couldn't wait to get back to his apartment. That's where he could play the stuff he really loved, the stuff that made him want to be a DJ in the first place—house music. But he had built a solid following and a livable income as a hip-hop DJ, so he kept soldiering on, living a dual identity. To the public, Yung Skeeter was a rising hip-hop DJ. In private, McFedries would shut that all out and go deep into house tracks.

Until a single night at the club when everything changed. In a split-moment decision, McFedries decided to smash his worlds together by playing a house track in the middle of a hip-hop set. At first, people in the club assumed the DJ had made a mistake and waited for the track to pass, but McFedries was already hooked. When he doubled down with more house music, the crowd became apoplectic. Nearly everyone left the dance floor. "But there was one person who stayed," he told me. "I ignored all of the annoyed faces and just made eye contact with her." Men with Jeter jerseys hurled insults, while others pleaded with the manager to "make it stop." One guy even offered McFedries $200 to switch back to hip-hop.

But McFedries tuned out the outrage and finished his house set. Needless to say, he wasn't invited back to that particular club. But it didn't matter—McFedries finally felt like he was expressing himself. He traded large hip-hop clubs for smaller, lower-paying house venues and slowly began to rebuild his reputation. Within a few years, he reached levels of success he'd never imagined as a hip-hop DJ. He performed at Coachella and became a close collaborator to Azealia Banks, Steve Aoki, and Katy Perry.

But years later, after he'd shifted from DJ to tech entrepreneur, he was getting nowhere with investors. That's when it hit him. The venture capitalists around the table were like the guys in the hip-hop club wearing Yankees caps. "I was making the same mistake all over again," McFedries told me. "I was expressing what they wanted to hear, not what I wanted to hear." That's when McFedries decided to change the track.

Instead of presenting slides—which never really fit his style—he started to speak the way he would to a friend. Less structured, more freestyle. "I know what we're building is different from what you're used to investing in," he would say. "But if we get this right, we could change the way storytelling works."

It didn't always work. Just like inside the hip-hop club, some people found it hard to embrace something new. But Kara Nortman at Upfront Ventures felt differently. Like the one house fan who remained on the dance floor, Nortman liked the direct, fresh approach. "I don't know if my partners will go along with this," she told McFedries. "But either way, there are some people I want to introduce you to."

Those introductions led McFedries to present in front of some of tech's most prominent backers, including Sequoia Capital. Within weeks of changing his pitch, McFedries went from being rejected by more than thirty investors to being backed by some of the biggest-name investors on the planet.

There's a difference between customizing your pitch and shoe-horning it into something it's not. Even if the shoehorning works and the backer says yes, it almost always leads to issues downstream. Investors pull out when the roadmap isn't what they expected. Films get axed in post-production because there wasn't a shared vision in pre-production. R&D projects get derailed in phase 2 because the vision wasn't fully expressed during phase 1.

One of the more important lessons I've had to learn as a founder is that most people aren't going to like my idea, and that's okay, because what I really need are a few people to *love* it. Just as an artist needs only a few galleries to feature her, a lawyer needs only a couple of partners to advocate for his promotion, and a screenwriter needs only one studio to say yes.

In an effort to get the word out about his global education nonprofit, Pencils of Promise, Adam Braun rented a thirty-five-foot RV to visit college campuses around the country. The first stop was Oklahoma State University, a school with thirty-five thousand students. There, Braun delivered his speech to five people, four of whom were with him in the RV. But like DJ Yung Skeeter, Adam Braun focused on the one person—a student named Chelsea Canada—and gave his presentation with just as much enthusiasm as if the room had been packed. By the time Braun and his crew were back on the road, his sole audience member had already launched the nonprofit's first college campus club.[7] Years later, Pencils of Promise has chapters around the globe, but Braun's goal has remained the same—find one person in every room, and convert them into the next Chelsea Canada.

After being rejected by every investor I initially pitched, I learned there are always more investors out there. Just as there are always more fellowship programs, government grants, and art exhibitions. Even inside big company cultures, I've watched creative people pitch their ideas to multiple different divisions before finding a sponsor. Once you realize the power of the passionate few, you no longer need to bend yourself into something that doesn't feel like you.

Letting go of my ego saved my startup. Earlier I mentioned we were struggling to make payroll. If I didn't secure partnerships and endorsements fast, we would be forced to shut down. As a health app that was delivered through the iPhone, the company we wanted to partner with the most was Apple. So you can imagine how thrilled I was when I got invited to the company headquarters to present Rise to some of Apple's senior executives. Shortly before my drive to Cupertino I received a message from the Apple team informing me that CEO Tim Cook—who once said, "Improving health will be Apple's greatest contribution to mankind"—would likely be in the room.

I wish I could tell you this news filled me with enthusiasm and energy. Instead it filled me with terror and dread. By the time I pulled into a parking spot at Apple HQ, I felt like I was going to have a panic attack.

Film directors often describe the brief period before they yell "Action!" as "the moment before the moment." What happens during those seconds can be as influential as the weeks, months, and years of preparation leading to them. It's that moment in the lobby before an interview, that moment at your desk before a key presentation, that moment before the doors open to your art exhibit.

Sitting in my car, in that moment before I walked into Apple's headquarters, I realized something—while the stakes were high, my ego had elevated them to almost mythological proportions. The outcome of the meeting felt like life or death.

Jerry Colonna, CEO and co-founder of Reboot.io Inc. and the author of *Reboot: Leadership and the Art of Growing Up,* once taught me that most of the fear we feel is self-induced. But we can see this only when, instead of pushing the fear away, we pull it in and examine it more closely. So, minutes before my presentation, I took out a piece of paper and tried a counterintuitive technique Colonna taught me. Here's how it went.

At the top of the page, I wrote:

"You are going to blow this meeting."

Then, instead of pushing that thought away, I asked myself: if that happened, then what?

"Then your company is going to fail," I wrote.

If that happened, then what?

"Everyone is going to lose their jobs."

And if that happened, then what?

"No one is ever going to want to invest in or work with you ever again."

And if that happened, then what?

"You are going to become miserable...your wife is going to leave you. And you're going to die alone."

That was rock bottom.

Now, you would think an exercise like this would make a frightened person even more terrified. But it didn't. In fact, it allowed me to see just how high my ego had raised the stakes of this meeting. No wonder I was panicked; buried inside my head was an idea that if I blew this meeting, I would lose my family.

A. J. Jacobs, editor at large for *Esquire* magazine, says, "If you can make your thoughts clear to yourself, then another part of your brain can take a closer look." Jacobs told me he'll sometimes talk to himself because "if I hear myself say something crazy out loud, another part of me can say, 'Oh, that *is* absurd.'"

The further you go down your "then what?" list, the more closely you can take a look at the fear behind the fear—and untangle thoughts that simply don't belong. The fear of public speaking doesn't stem from blowing that speech but from a trail of events we imagine might happen as a result.

By the time I got out of my car in the Apple parking lot, Colonna's exercise had helped me let go of my ego. If they didn't like the idea of Rise, I'd find another partner who did. I walked into the building (and through multiple security checkpoints) with a higher level of clarity and confidence than I could remember feeling. A couple of months after the meeting, Apple named Rise a Best New App of the Year.

CONCLUSION:

THE GAME OF NOW

When I was in my early twenties, I took my first trip to Silicon Valley. It was the start of the 2000s and the hot companies were Yahoo!, eBay, and Hotmail. I was fascinated by that world but, unfortunately, didn't know anyone there. So, I naively started cold-calling all the household names in tech—including prominent investors like Vinod Khosla and John Doerr. Unsurprisingly, I didn't get through. But while searching for their contact information, I stumbled upon an article about a restaurant called Buck's of Woodside where valley insiders ate their power breakfasts. The article featured a photo of the owner, Jamis MacNiven, dressed in a bowling shirt with glasses, a warm and inviting smile on his face.

With nothing to lose, I reached out cold to MacNiven, asking if I could swing by his restaurant and introduce myself. "Come on by," he said.

When I walked through the door at Buck's, I took a step back out and double-checked the address. *This* was the elite meeting place for venture capitalists and entrepreneurs? One of the first things you see is a giant model Statue of Liberty wearing a sombrero and holding an ice cream cone. It felt like a place where kids celebrate their birthdays, not a hot spot for industry titans.

I was seated by the window, mesmerized by the memorabilia and knickknacks hanging from the ceiling, when MacNiven came out to greet me, sliding into my booth. He was wearing a short-sleeved Hawaiian shirt and crumpled khakis. The guy the *Wall Street Journal* described as a power broker looked straight out of Margaritaville.

As MacNiven and I scarfed down pumpkin pancakes, the November breakfast special, he gave me a sit-down tour of the place. "That's where Marc Andreessen got his funding for Netscape," he said, pointing to the left. "Hotmail was founded at that table," he added, nodding straight ahead. "PayPal was funded over there."

MacNiven's tour took my attention from the decorations— from the kitschy Buddhas and encased Nancy and Ronald Reagan slippers—to the people sitting around us, the one-on-one breakfasts. What I saw in that moment, twenty years ago, surprised and inspired me. What I saw ultimately drove me to write this book.

Nearly every table had a similar pattern: On one side, a professionally dressed man with graying hair. On the other side, someone who looked a lot like . . . me. My age, my level of experience—wearing the same kind of hoodie I'd be wearing if it were a Saturday.

I wanted to know what the hoodies were saying to the suits. Lost in thought, I was startled when MacNiven said, "They're pitching their ideas." I wondered whether to say what I wanted to say. Finally, I forced it out. "But they're so young. I mean...they're my age." MacNiven took a sip from his "Dukakis for Governor" coffee mug and looked out the window. It seemed like he was debating whether or not to tell me the truth. Would it be too much for a twenty-one-year-old from the Midwest to handle?

In that moment, I was reminded of the scene in *The Matrix* where Morpheus holds out a red pill and a blue pill. MacNiven leaned across the table, looked me directly in the eyes, and pointed out the window. "The people who run this place...they're all your age." I felt a lump in my throat. Red pill.

My mind raced the entire flight back to Detroit. I kept thinking back to the hoodies at the diner who seemed to understand something that I didn't. Something I wouldn't comprehend until years later. That there are two types of people in this world. There are those who play the Game of Someday and those who play the Game of Now.

Every backable person I've met, at some point in their career, learns to play the Game of Now. When Brian Grazer was trying to break into Hollywood, he convinced Lew Wasserman, one of the industry's most influential rainmakers, to give him some career advice. Two minutes into the meeting, while Grazer was sharing his background, Wasserman interrupted and said, "All right, enough! Pull out a piece of paper." Then Wasserman told him to start writing—to stop talking about writing, and just write. That piece of paper led to *Splash*, starring Tom Hanks, and Grazer soon after formed Imagine Entertainment with Ron Howard. He looks back at that single act—writing down his idea—as a moment that would define his career. The moment he began to play the Game of Now.

When I speak to audiences, I like to start with a quick

exercise. I'll say, "Stand up if you have a creative idea. Anything new—it can be simple or groundbreaking. It can be an idea for a new product, a new process...anything you think might make a *meaningful* difference."

Within a few moments, almost everyone is standing.

Then I'll ask people to remain standing "if you have *not* shared that idea."

More than half the audience continues to stand.

I've been doing this exercise for years, and the result is always the same. Meanwhile companies spend billions of dollars hiring outside consultants and high-priced think tanks to come up with ideas that already exist in the minds of their own employees. Their genius remains hidden in plain sight.

Mahatma Gandhi said, "The difference between what we do and what we are capable of doing would suffice to solve most of the world's problems." Now, more than ever, we need good people to stop playing the Game of Someday and start playing the Game of Now. That begins with you.

The craziest ideas—the ones that are most likely to change the world—are often the hardest ones to sell. But that doesn't mean we stop trying. We build the skills and invest the energy to make ourselves backable. And we realize, as all backable people eventually do, that when you get dismissed, there is always another room.

And if that's not enough to convince you to play the Game of Now, then consider this: even when our ideas don't reach their intended destination, they still touch and inspire people along the way. Truth be told, Rise didn't become the powerhouse I thought it could be. When we sold to One Medical, it was a nice outcome for our team and a solid return for our shareholders—but I signed the final paperwork with mixed feelings. I had hoped we could have been more.

But in the years after the sale, I was approached by people who were building their own version of Rise. I got asked to share what I learned from my experience inside classrooms and hospitals. At a conference hosted by *Fortune* magazine an entrepreneur spoke about a service he built that dramatically shrinks the cost of mental health care. When he was asked how he came up with the idea, he said, "I was inspired by a service called Rise." He didn't know I was in the audience, and his comment caught me off guard, because we had never met. When we play the Game of Now, the direct result of what we do isn't the end of the story.

I now know the three words that hold most of us back from the Game of Now: "I'm not ready." I'm not ready to start my business; I'm not ready to write that proposal; I'm not ready to speak my mind. We've all felt that way. Even as I type the final words of this manuscript, there's a faint, sometimes loud, voice saying, Why you? Why would anyone want to read what you have to say?

But after spending over five years interviewing and studying people who've changed the world, something occurred to me: none of them were ready. A hedge fund manager with zero entrepreneurial track record wasn't necessarily ready to build an online bookseller. Friends from design school weren't prepared to disrupt the hospitality industry. A fifteen-year-old from Stockholm wasn't ready to lead an environmental movement. But today, Amazon is not only the world's largest bookstore, but the biggest online retailer. Hundreds of thousands of people check into an Airbnb every single day.[1] And Greta Thunberg has been named the youngest ever Person of the Year by *Time* magazine.

By becoming Ford Motor Company's first female engineer,

my mom created possibilities not just for herself, but for everyone around her, including her family. In 1967, her car broke down outside Ann Arbor, so she found a telephone booth and searched the phone book for the most common Indian name she could think of. The guy who answered was my father, Subhash Gupta. They were married within a year and had two sons—Sanjay and me.

We grew up in an almost boringly safe suburb, never experiencing anything close to the conditions Mom experienced. And yet somehow Sanjay and I both inherited her refugee mentality—this strange mix of impermanence and optimism. If we had a goal, she'd push us to figure out how, and figure it out *now*. The Game of Someday wasn't allowed.

Years later, my brother had the idea that a practicing physician from Detroit could be on national television reporting the news. Despite the fact that Sanjay had zero on-air experience, Mom told him to believe in himself and figure out a way. Just as she had found her way to a hiring manager at Ford, he found his way to an interview with the executives and producers at CNN.

Sanjay knew becoming a television reporter was a long shot, but he'd taken the incubation time to prepare for that moment. He steered straight into the objection that he didn't have on-camera experience and pointed out that as a practicing physician, he had a much more authentic connection with patients—his central character—than a typical reporter might have. He was already immersed in the stories CNN wanted to tell, and he had earned secrets to share.

A few weeks after I met Jamis MacNiven inside his quirky restaurant, Dr. Sanjay Gupta made his debut on CNN. For the past twenty years I've proudly watched my big brother report the news—from 9/11 to COVID-19. He keeps reminding us that we're all in this together and reminding me to keep playing the Game of Now.

That's why Sanjay was my first call when I decided to move back to Michigan to run for Congress. In 2016, Donald Trump had won the state by fewer than eleven thousand votes. As a Democrat, I wanted to go home and help turn the tide.

Running for office is, in many ways, like building a startup. You're moving fast, making lots of mistakes, and always running out of funding. But we had an important asset—we had Mom. At the age of seventy-six, she came out of retirement to join my campaign, energetically knocking on more doors than any other member of our staff. The night of the election, when it was too close to call, she stayed up later than even Leena and me to wait for the final result.

The next morning I woke up to learn that I had lost. As I lay in bed, staring at the results on my screen, I could hear Mom downstairs making her morning cup of Indian chai. Her gentle sounds transported me back to my childhood, when all I wanted to do was please her. It felt like the morning after a parent-teacher conference—and I imagined, for a moment, how proud she would have been if the election had turned out differently. If I could have played the Game of Now she taught me, and won.

Slowly making my way down the stairs, I braced myself for the disappointment in her voice. But when I walked into the kitchen, Mom said nothing. Instead she put down her mug, walked over, and wrapped her arms around me.

The Game of Now may not always lead to success. But the opposite of success isn't failure; it's boredom. So let's play this game together. Let's fight for the ideas that make us come alive and inspire good people to join us in the game. Let's experience moments that we'll cherish forever, even when it hurts.

Because you are ready.

ACKNOWLEDGMENTS

When I first met Carlye Adler, she had already written books alongside highly distinguished thinkers and business leaders. I was neither, so I was surprised and delighted when she agreed to be my writing partner. If it weren't for Carlye this book would be a patchwork of disconnected thoughts. She gave it a unified spine, so the ideas inside could have a soul.

Dikran Ornekian joined our team in our final ten months of this project. It's a rare gift in life when your best friend becomes your lifelong collaborator. Since the day we met on the Little League field outside of Village Oaks elementary, I've watched Dikran creatively bring boring things to life. That's exactly what he did in these pages.

Joel Stein, Andrew Waller, and Campbell Schnebly took the time to review early drafts of the book, and give us fresh ideas to make it stronger.

Phil Marino, our editor, pushed this work to its full potential. I originally pitched *Backable* as a book primarily for entrepreneurs, but Phil always knew it could be bigger than that. He, along with the many talented people at Little, Brown, gave me the confidence and space to think bigger. A special thank you to Bruce Nichols for taking this book, and Claudia Connal and Faye Robson in the UK for poring over these pages and priming them for a global audience.

David Vigliano is an agent's agent. He has a sixth sense for the publishing industry, and watching him work is like watching an elite athlete on the field. I'm grateful to him for taking me on as a client when I had no track record or evidence that I could write.

Bob Thomas and his team at the Worldwide Speakers Group took an early bet on *Backable* and helped us put the topic in front of wonderful audiences around the world. Even during a pandemic, they helped steer this project through uncertain times.

This book is rooted in my story, and there were many people who made it possible. Mom and Dad taught me how to set goals and work hard. Sanjay taught me how to constantly reexamine whether those goals match who I truly am. Andy Mahoney has been my business and life coach for nearly ten years. Without his encouragement, I never would have wandered down the path of writing a book.

In the midst of a pandemic, my daughters, Samara "Sammy" and Serena "Zuzu," created a home filled with joy. Writing is by nature isolating work, but because of them I never felt alone. Sammy, age eight, would draw me pictures for *Backable*'s cover. Serena, age three, would listen to me read rough drafts, then look me in the eyes and say, "Good job, Daddy." I suspect that neither of them will really need this book, but I hope they know how important they've been to its completion.

Leena always believed in *Backable*, even when I didn't. You could replace *"Backable"* with "me" and that last sentence would still be true. I am who I am...because she took a chance on me.

APPENDIX 1:
CHAPTER SUMMARIES

STEP 1: CONVINCE YOURSELF FIRST

- **Schedule Incubation Time.** Pitching your idea prematurely often leads to a lukewarm response that can dampen or even destroy enthusiasm. Remember it's not charisma that convinces people; it's conviction. You can't get others to buy in on an idea that you are not completely sold on yourself. Chef Aduriz shuts his restaurant down for three months every year to build confidence in new recipes before sharing them with the world. Remember, most new ideas are not killed inside conference rooms. They're killed inside hallways and break rooms, where they are shared before they are developed. So give your idea the incubation time it needs to grow.
- **Steer into Objections.** Put yourself in the shoes of a potential backer and anticipate three key objections to your idea. When pitching, don't avoid those

objections; lean into them. Avoidance only leads to more questions later, and the possibility that the backer tunes out the rest of your pitch. When Reid Hoffman was first pitching LinkedIn, the company didn't have a dime of revenue. But instead of veering away from the revenue question, he hit it directly, showcasing ways the startup could make money down the line. Get ahead of these criticisms, and you'll gain credibility for the stronger parts of your pitch.

- **Throwaway Work.** Accept the fact that, in the early days of a new idea, most of what you produce will not be usable. But throwaway work is not a waste of time; it's part of the process. Salman Rushdie didn't get inspired to write every day; he simply sat down and did the work, knowing full well that the majority of it would end up in a trash bin. But what remained were tiny pearls that, when strung together, formed sentences, paragraphs, and eventually books.

- **Measure Your Emotional Runway.** Intellectual interest is important, but it's rarely enough—you need to be emotionally invested in your idea. Bringing something new into the world requires a tremendous amount of stamina because you're on the receiving end of doubts, conflicts, and deadlines. Conviction can be replenished only by your own passion for the idea. Lin-Manuel Miranda says that ideas like *Hamilton* take years to create so "you really have to fall in love" to invest the effort it requires. When considering a concept, don't just figure out if it fits the market—figure out if it truly fits you.

STEP 2: CAST A CENTRAL CHARACTER

- **Choose One Person.** We emotionally connect to people, not to concepts. *The 4-Hour Workweek* sold millions of copies, but Tim Ferriss wrote it for two specific friends who felt trapped by their jobs. The best ideas root us in the story of a central character so that we connect with the concept on a human level.

- **Create a Storyboard.** Share your customer's step-by-step experience. Kirsten Green had zero interest in the Dollar Shave Club until she listened to Michael Dubin talk through his customer's painful experience inside a pharmacy. Storyboards are an "empathy bridge" between your backer and your customer. They deeply connect with the person we're trying to serve. To see what they see, to feel what they feel.

- **Keep Your Character in Sight.** Groupon and Uber built cultures around a central character, but seemed to unravel when they lost sight of the person they meant to serve. Don't cast a central character and then cut them halfway through your story. Keep them as the hero, and you'll keep everyone around you inspired.

STEP 3: FIND AN EARNED SECRET

- **Go Beyond Google.** Great ideas tend to stem from an earned secret—a hidden insight you learn through firsthand experience. When coming up with your idea, imagine yourself as James Cameron, diving the shipwreck of the *Titanic*. Look for things that can't be found from behind a desk. As Brian Grazer told me, "I want an idea that is based on a surprise insight. Not something I could find through a Google search."

- **Intoxicate Them with Effort.** To convince a reluctant Howard Stern that writing a new book would not be "torture," publishing executive Jonathan Karp and his team combed through hundreds upon hundreds of Stern's interview transcripts and came back to Stern with a preassembled book. By going the extra mile, Karp essentially willed a bestseller into existence. Remember, how you arrive at an idea can be as memorable and important as the idea itself. I was reluctant, even embarrassed, to let investors know that I recruited early customers for Rise by standing outside Weight Watchers meetings. And yet that turned out to be a part of the pitch they loved most.

STEP 4: MAKE IT FEEL INEVITABLE

- **Be an Armchair Anthropologist.** A typical pitch communicates that an idea is new. A backable pitch communicates that an idea is *inevitable*. The Airbnb founders had to convince investors that people would be open to sharing their home with a stranger. Rather than trying to tell investors how they thought the world should be, they showed how the world was already headed in that direction. Inside Airbnb's original pitch deck was a critical slide showing that home sharing was already a growing phenomenon on Couchsurfing.com and Craigslist.

- **With or Without Us.** Our fear of betting on the wrong idea is twice as powerful as our pleasure from betting on the right one. Neutralize fear with fear—create a sense of FOMO around your idea by showing backers how it is inevitable. Sam Schwartz sold Comcast on Xfinity Mobile by making the argument that this idea would inevitably be built—either by Comcast or one of its competitors. The only thing equally powerful to missing is missing out.

- **Show Momentum.** Without momentum, the case for inevitability can fall flat. Show your backer that a shift is inevitable *and* that you've already made progress to get ahead of the curve. Andy Dunn made a convincing argument to investors that Bonobos was an inevitable idea. But it was his early sales—moving pants out of the trunk of a car—that pushed investors over the hump. Without that tiny bit of momentum, Dunn says investors never would have backed him.

- **Have Vision, Not Visions.** Steve Jobs didn't create a trend with the iPhone; he accelerated one. Wayne Gretzky once said, "I skate to where the puck is going to be." Most people we consider visionaries are simply skating to where the puck is inevitably heading.

STEP 5: FLIP OUTSIDERS TO INSIDERS

- **Share What It Could Be, Not How It Has to Be.** Sharing every detail of your plan can make it feel like your idea is locked in stone and tends to shut the backer out of the creative process. Backers who get most excited about an idea feel like they're on the inside of an idea. Jimmy Page agreed to be part of a documentary film because the director showed him that they'd "tell this story together." Remember, decisions that affect your career often happen when you're not even in the room. That's why when we pitch, we're not looking for just a backer, we're looking for an advocate—someone who can invest in our ideas with equal enthusiasm.

- **The Story of Us.** If you're already on a clear path to success, that might make you a weaker candidate for the MacArthur Foundation's "genius grant." MacArthur wants to have an actual impact on your career outcome, which is the case for most backers. So understand and communicate how your gaps and your backer's strengths come together. Instead of showing them how you'll succeed alone, show them why you will succeed together.

- **Make *Them* the Hero.** We don't typically win people over in one conversation, but through a series of interactions that builds trust and confidence. Even if they pass on your initial pitch, there's still an opportunity to win them over. Brian Wood impressed Pentagon officials when he returned with a revised prototype that utilized their feedback. So when a backer says no, find out why they passed, listen carefully to their feedback, and—when you return—show them how you've specifically addressed their concerns.

- **Share Just Enough.** When designer Jake Knapp ditched his high-fidelity mockups and shared hand-drawn sketches instead, people rallied around his vision. Share just enough to get the essence of your idea across, then open up the conversation. Keep things elastic so that you can fold in possibilities that come up inside the room.

STEP 6: PLAY EXHIBITION MATCHES

- **No Venue Is Too Small.** Use low-stakes practice sessions to prepare for high-stakes moments. Be like Jerry Seinfeld and take every opportunity to practice, no matter the size of the audience. If a friend asks about your idea, instead of giving them the overview, ask them to listen to your pitch. And no matter whom you're practicing in front of, give them the real version. No director's commentary. It might feel awkward at first, but the real benefits come when you practice as if it's the actual pitch. When no venue is too small, the world becomes your stadium.
- **Be Willing to Be Embarrassed.** Most people want to avoid negative feedback; it's a natural instinct. But long-term success often comes from short-term embarrassment. Your first few exhibition matches will be your worst ones. Accept this and get them out of the way with low-risk audiences.
- **Don't Ask, "What Do You Think?"** The goal of an exhibition match is to get the most direct feedback possible. Like Dr. Tom Lee, treat questions like medical instruments to probe beneath the surface for the most useful information. After explaining an idea to a friend, I'll often ask them to explain it back to me in their own words. Not only does that help me understand whether

the concept is actually landing; it also helps me pick up new ways to explain my own idea.

- **Build Your Backable Circle.** Don't rely on just one person to help you with your pitch. Instead surround yourself with a small group of trusted people who bring different perspectives and play different roles to get you ready for a backer. Embrace your "Cheddar"—the person who will deliberately poke holes in your ideas, sometimes in a way that is deeply annoying. Because, in the end, Cheddar is the one who's going to help you get ahead of a backer's objections.

- **The Rule of 21.** Like great jazz musicians, backable people anticipate something will go wrong during the pitch. But they know they have built enough "recovery muscle" to pull through it well. This level of confidence comes with lots of practice. While it might sound like overkill, practicing something twenty-one times will make your "recovery muscle" strong enough to overcome any interruption or interrogation. And counter to conventional thinking, being this practiced will make you more, not less, natural and present.

- **Reboot Your Style.** After losing a primary election for Congress, Barack Obama reinvented his style and ran for president. Your exhibition matches might lead you to see that your style isn't working. Instead of throwing away your dream, have the courage to reinvent your style. Every successful person has done this. Want proof? Search for an old speech of someone you admire and notice how their communication style has changed. Reinvention is an essential part of the backable process.

STEP 7: LET GO OF YOUR EGO

- **Show, Don't Tell.** People are far more compelling when they're showing their idea rather than simply describing it. When the pizza-app founder went from his pitch deck to demo'ing his app, a switch flipped and he lit up. So whenever possible, shift from presentation mode to "huddle mode," where you and your backer are looking at something together. Huddle mode tends to put you in a place where you're more natural, comfortable, and confident.

- **Forget Yourself.** When you feel the spotlight on you, turn it toward your idea. Remember, you're not representing yourself inside the room; you're representing the person you want to serve. When Liz started to think of herself as an agent for her customer, she stopped sweating through her clothes and captivated the entire boardroom. Seeing yourself as an advocate for your customer takes you outside your own head...so like Charlie Parker you can forget yourself and just wail.

- **Find the Passionate Few.** Not everyone is going to like your idea—and that's okay, because all you need are a few who love it. Find the passionate few who believe in who you are and what you're trying to create. There's a difference between customizing your pitch and shoehorning it into something it's not. Stay true to your idea and remember there's always another backer out there.

APPENDIX 2:
HIGHLIGHTS FROM SELECT INTERVIEWS WITH BACKABLE PEOPLE

My goal was to give you a book that you could absorb quickly and put into practice immediately. I hope it worked. The hardest part of being succinct was cutting hundreds of pages, even ones that could be useful. That's why Carlye and I wanted to share a handful of the interviews that kept coming up during our conversations. We've selected the most valuable moments from these interviews and edited them lightly for clarity. Many of these insights didn't make it into the core of the book, but they continue to make us think.

KIRSTEN GREEN, VENTURE CAPITALIST

Kirsten is the founder of Forerunner Ventures. Forerunner has raised more than $1 billion and backed nearly one hundred companies, including early winners Warby Parker, Bonobos, and Glossier. She has been repeatedly included on the *Forbes* Midas List and the World's 100 Most Powerful Women. When I was creating Rise, struggling to figure out how to build a brand, people would always tell me, "You have to talk to Kirsten." Eventually I got the chance.

> "The business of venture capital asks us to be looking for what is possible today but highly relevant tomorrow. To find that balance you have to have both a vision for the future and then a practical approach to what you are going to do in the next twelve months. When I think about something that's backable, we are looking for the balance of both."

Carlye: You took a bet on Michael Dubin and Dollar Shave Club. Can you tell us that story?

Kirsten: Another co-investor asked me had I seen this company, Dollar Shave Club. I replied, "No, what is it?" They give a very brief description, essentially razors cheaper online. And I said, "Oh, I don't think that's for me."

Carlye: Why not?

Kirsten: Low-ticket dollar items are generally hard businesses given low-margin dollars available to invest in things that we think are important, including, of course, your foundation, infrastructure, but also great customer service and supporting brand building. More importantly, probably, was the hyper-competitive landscape, with Gillette being a juggernaut with both a considerable balance sheet and marketing prowess. Gillette is a formidable competitor.

Carlye: So, it doesn't sound as if you were very interested. What changed?

Kirsten: Ironically, two days, maybe three days later I was at a dinner and I was introduced to Michael Dubin.

Carlye: Randomly?

Kirsten: Well, kind of randomly, because it's all a small eco-system and this dinner had been planned with thirty people as a mixture of investors and entrepreneurs. This is in San Francisco in February of 2012. Within ten minutes of talking to Michael, in the back of my mind, I felt, "How do I get this guy a check? I have to be in business with him."

Carlye: Wow, what changed your mind?

Kirsten: It's interesting, in the context of what you're writing, because it was the way Michael brought it to life that was everything in this scenario. Without that overlay, it didn't capture my imagination.

Suneel: What do you remember from those ten minutes?

Kirsten: This is six years ago, seven years ago now, so forgive me, I can't repeat it verbatim, but it went like this: "Oh, so you're selling razors?" And he immediately went into a narrative around the customer, demonstrating that he had a viewpoint and a read on the consumer that he was looking to serve, an understanding of how they were evolving and how their preferences were changing. He articulated that "there are guys taking ownership over their purchase decisions, becoming more active consumers. Like everybody else, they're reading, and getting more information online. And some part of that is health, wellness, grooming, taking care of yourself, and what exists or doesn't exist in that category. And if those two things get them to go to Walgreens and think about their shaving products, then they're met with resistance because everything on this shelf looks like yesteryear. It doesn't speak to them like other brands and products that they're interacting with. And maybe it's under lock and key, so there's legitimate friction." And then he suggests, "I think the whole thing needs to be reimagined in the context of the market today and this customer today. This customer wants to shop in the privacy and convenience of their own home or digital device, they want to be talked to in a way that connects with them."

Suneel: Did that conversation change your perception about razor blades as a business?

Kirsten: It wasn't about razors; it was about the customer, as well as how the business models in the space were being challenged. And I [can't] even remember whether it was in that first conversation or a follow-up conversation, which is "Why razors?" And then I heard the story about the razors and he's like, on some level the razors are a great way to start the conversation because it's something that everybody uses. It's debatable whether everybody uses a face cleanser or moisturizers or sunscreen, but most everybody uses a razor and I think that everybody has at one time or another questioned the cost of a razor. So, it's a conversation starter, but the bigger idea is to solve his grooming routine.

Carlye: I love that you knew within ten minutes of talking to him. Does it go down that way usually?

Kirsten: This is probably not the right thing to write in your book, but between us, a lot of times it does. A lot of times you kind of know what you're passionate about and excited about. Really, does anyone come in with something you've never heard any inkling about before? A lot of times you have some proclivity toward it, whether you consciously knew it or not.

Carlye: It sounds like he just painted it so beautifully and there was so much momentum, it was almost unstoppable. But is there a way that this could go wrong, that the vision could seem too big, that it's not believable?

Kirsten: There's always a way everything could go wrong, right? The business of venture capital asks us to be looking for what is possible today but highly relevant tomorrow. So where are things directionally headed? And that has to be something that you imagine revealing itself over time. You have to be able to look today and say there's enough buy-in, there's enough reason to believe that some critical mass of people will start to adopt that. To find that balance you have to have both a vision for the future and then a practical approach to what you are going to do in the next twelve months. When I think about something that's backable, we are looking for the balance of both.

Suneel: How do you balance the dream with the plan?

Kirsten: Deliberately. You come in and you have a big vision. You're able to talk about some shifting in the market, some start of a tailwind that you notice and some way that you're imagining how the future unfolds and where your company fits into that. And then you think about how to translate that into the earliest stages of action. "We're raising X amount of money because the first thing we're going to do is prove that we can hire four people and do a proof of concept of this product and test it in the market." Then it's, "Okay, we've done some tests in the market, we've gotten some early customer feedback, we now have enough data points that we know exactly where we're going to direct dollars to reiterate on the product, or to iterate on the product, and we're going to start investing in marketing, we're going to start investing in sales channels." Then I know that you have a vision, but you are grounded in the fact that there is a lot of heavy lifting and work that needs to happen from going from A to B and you've thought about what are the few things that you can prove in this chapter of business.

Suneel: It seems like that could be an outline for any founder giving a pitch. Why do you think that format is so rarely used?

Kirsten: I think sometimes when you're very close to the business, it's hard to figure out what are the most important things to pull out, and where are you too far into the details. So you end up using precious space in your pitch on things that could be follow-up conversation as opposed to answering the question of "Is this a visionary idea?" I think you can undershare in that pursuit in an effort to be concise.

Carlye: How do some people present in a way that's not going to be backable? Are there common mistakes that you're seeing?

Kirsten: Few people present a whole picture. Everybody has strengths, and the most comfortable thing is to lean into those, when you're operating a business, as well as when you're pitching a business. And so sometimes the pitch becomes lopsided. One person presents an opportunity with a very tactical, functional, numbers-driven approach and I may feel less inspired or unconvinced that this founder is going to be able to compel people toward those results. On the flip side, sometimes people overindex into the creativity and are almost all about the aesthetic of the presentation or about the grand vision, and there's just not enough meat on the bones relative to the tactics. And so, as an investor, it gives us a real window into, "Okay, what are the things you need to fill in around?" And so the next line of questioning centers on trying to understand "How much self-awareness does this person have?"

Suneel: Are you able to coach people who are more numbers, meat-on-the-bone-type thinkers to actually think about the vision?

Kirsten: I think people can be brought along in their vision, and become more confident in being expansive with it. But most of the time there was always a nugget of it there. When I think about a visionary in the context of the questions you have been posing, I'm thinking about somebody who is recognizing shifts that are happening and aims to play into that with a better offering. This person is able to connect dots and then push them forward in a way that's not obvious. That's rare to find and I don't think that everybody we've ever backed had that day one when they came in. They demonstrated an ambition to be part of the category and enough raw intelligence, curiosity, passion, that I can make a leap to believe that they will uncover things along the way that further and build that vision. Nobody knows all the answers on day one. I'm working to really understand if somebody is going to be looking for ways to have a bigger impact with their business over time.

PETER CHERNIN, ENTERTAINMENT EXECUTIVE AND INVESTOR

Peter served as the chairman and CEO of 20th Century Fox when the studio produced two of the highest-grossing films of all time—*Titanic* and *Avatar*. One of our favorite stories is about how James Cameron initially pitched Peter on the idea for *Titanic*. After leaving Fox, Peter formed the Chernin Group, which has produced films like *Oblivion* and *Ford v Ferrari* and invests in technology companies including Pandora, the Athletic, and Twitter. We talked about what it takes to become backable across different industries from both sides of the table.

> "You need to do whatever it takes to convince me, or the powers that be. If there's an idea that you really believe in, you need to do whatever it takes to get us to do it. You should burn down my car in the parking lot, if you think I'm making a stupid mistake. And if you don't...it's your fault for giving up too easily."

Suneel: You began your career as a book editor, so maybe that's a good place to begin. Have you ever thought about writing a book yourself?

Peter: Seems too hard. It's like real work.

Suneel: People are pitching you every day. I'm interested in hearing about the types of ideas that you like and don't like. What kind of ideas turn you off the most?

Peter: Anything that feels cynical. What I mean by that is something where you go, "Well, this is kind of stupid, but the idiots out there will like it." That's my single biggest hot button.

The next thing that sets me off is "ordinary." People are looking for excitement in their lives. Human nature suggests that people are looking for discovery. Humans are curious, they're impatient, they're bored easily. People are constantly looking for something that feels new and exciting to them, which is why I'm concerned about ordinary. What I always picture in my mind is someone's reaction when they hear something new; if their reaction is "been there, done that," it's just like ten other books or ten other movies or ten other restaurants, that always feels like the kiss of death.

And conversely the reaction "Wow, what is that? That sounds weird, that sounds exciting, that sounds interesting. I don't want to miss out on that. I want to be the first person to experience that." Those feel like the best kinds of ideas.

Suneel: Does that put the person who's coming up with ideas and pitching them in a tough spot, because the biggest, craziest ideas are also the hardest ideas to pitch?

Peter: Sure. But so what? They're certainly the hardest, but I think by definition they are the ideas that the best creative people and the best entrepreneurs are most excited about. And the easiest way to pitch those really difficult ideas is to convey your own excitement. You need to figure out ways to convince other people why it's so exciting to you and to get them excited about it.

Suneel: What role does enthusiasm play during a pitch? There are just certain people obviously who wear excitement on their sleeve, but what if you're not one of those people? What if you tend to be more of a type B personality, quiet, but you've got bold ideas, what then?

Peter: I've come to believe that enthusiasm is an extraordinary skill, and an extraordinarily infectious skill. The best thing parents can do is to raise their children in a way where they generally feel enthusiastic about things. I think that people pitch, sell, discuss things they believe, in very different ways. And you have to be true to yourself.

I think that people sometimes make a mistake saying "I'm a little shy and therefore I'm not good at selling." I don't think all selling or all pitching is by definition overwhelmingly extroverted. You are most convincing in the ways that you are true to yourself. If you are an extraordinarily analytical person, you're likely to be most convincing by being analytical about why you believe in something. If you're an extraordinarily ebullient, enthusiastic person, that's likely to be the best way.

Quieter people—and you may or may not believe this, I probably count myself in the same way—are most convincing by sincerity. By trying to sincerely express what excites you about something. A lot of people who are not overwhelmingly gregarious think, "I can't sell well, that's not my personality." But in general the most convincing salespeople or pitchers are those who are super sincere and they're thoughtful and give thought to trying to express why something excites them.

Suneel: That's interesting; you don't count yourself as being extroverted, and you're in a business that seems inherently extroverted. Were there things that you learned early on in your career about how to hold your own in a room?

Peter: No, I'm not sure I learned it. I think I had genuine enthusiasm for things I believe in, and I think I learned how to express that enthusiasm. For example, I never bullshit anybody in trying to express my enthusiasm. I've always tried to be fairly honest about why I believe in it, and what I think the risks are, and I think that honesty has ultimately been compelling, because people feel like, Wow, they're not trying to bullshit me. I think when people feel like they're being sold they tend to be a little defensive, protective, self-protective. So part of what I mean by sincerity is they're willing to say, "This is really risky, I may be wrong, but this is why I love this idea...These are the ways it will not work, but this is why I believe it will work." You build a lot of credibility doing that.

No one's trying to say, "Oh my God, this is the greatest idea ever, and I guarantee you it's going to work." Those are the worst pitches. Self-awareness I find really compelling. It's funny, we're talking about an investment right now. The way we were describing the entrepreneur was, "He's a little cocky, he's a little bit of a hustler, but what we like about him is he's got great self-awareness, and he's not trying to pretend he knows what he doesn't know." That ends up being compelling.

Carlye: Is this something that comes up often in successful pitches, this balance between self-doubt, self-awareness, self-deprecation?

Peter: I find that it immediately takes away the defensiveness that I'm being bullshitted. Let me tell you something, which isn't about pitching, but which I think is a lesson I learned really well. When we were making *Titanic*—which, when I said yes to it, was the most expensive movie ever made, so I'm already way out on a limb there. I said yes to it, I think about $110 or $115 million. And then we went $110 million over budget. So we went more over budget than any movie that had ever been made. My job at that point was chairman and CEO of the movie studio, and I reported to Rupert Murdoch. I developed a habit early on in the process where—and at that stage Rupert was living in California, and his office was right across the hall from me—whenever I heard bad news, and I was hearing a lot of bad news, I was hearing $3 to $5 million a week of bad news, I would run across the hall and tell him that bad news.

I'd say, "Look, this is what just happened, this is why it happened, this is what we're going to try and do about it. I'm not sure it's going to work, but this is what feels to me to be the right response." It turned out to be remarkably effective, because he never felt like I was trying to hide the problems from him. He always felt like I was being incredibly transparent about the problems. I wasn't saying, "Geez, I don't know what to do." I was saying, "This is what I think we should do." I wasn't saying, "I know all the answers." Because clearly I didn't.

Carlye: Why do you think that approach was so effective?

Peter: I think it bought me enormous credibility that I led with the problems. I've always said this to the people who worked for me: "You know what, don't worry about good news. Trust me, good news is going to find me. I want to know bad news immediately." And in some ways you're going to be evaluated by your openness and transparency about bad news. To the degree that you're transparent about it, and I believe in you, I'll be the biggest supporter you've ever had, and to the degree you hide bad news from me, I don't see how I can support you, because how do I possibly trust you? And while it's not a direct analogy, I do think there's a fair amount of that, that extends into the notion of pitching things, which is to the degree someone has credibility.

Look, by definition, you're taking a risk anytime you buy an idea. And if you can establish personal credibility, it removes a huge barrier. You establish personal credibility by being willing to be open and transparent about what the risks are, how you see the risks, what your concerns are. I believe the willingness to express nervousness and concerns about things is extraordinarily compelling. Because it suggests that someone is being thoughtful, it suggests that someone is being open and honest with me, it suggests that they're not just full of shit and saying everything's great, and it's a huge barrier you overcome, because if you haven't overcome that barrier, the person on the receiving end of an idea has to do all that work themselves. Do they really know the risks? Do I believe in them? Are they really honest with themselves? Are they going to be good partners when we go through rough patches together?

It's something that a lot of people who are selling don't really think about, but being transparent and being humble and being honest about your concerns buys you enormous credibility, and ultimately backing any idea is about credibility.

Suneel: So, when James Cameron was pitching you on *Titanic*, were these the same traits that you would have described in him?

Peter: Jim has that quality of any really great filmmaker of unbelievable confidence. The undertakings are so overwhelming that you have to have real confidence. He doesn't go into it saying, "My God, we could go $100 million over budget." He believes that he's got confidence and can figure it out. But I remember the *Titanic* pitch was really interesting. In a lot of ways the most memorable pitch I was ever part of. Jim came and sat in my office, we sat on a couch with a coffee table between us, and we talked for probably three hours about *Titanic*. I would say 60 percent of it was talking about the historical event, and 30 or 40 percent of it was talking about the movie itself.

He had such extraordinary knowledge about the ship, which was fascinating. For example, if you were a woman in first class, you had basically a 99.9 percent chance of survival; well over 99 percent of the women in first class survived. If you were a male in steerage you had about a 30 percent chance of survival. People on one side of the ship, I forget whether it was the port or starboard, had about a 40 percent better survival rate than people on the other side of the ship. Mostly because one side was pretty well organized in launching life rafts, and getting people into them, and the other side was pure chaos.

Suneel: When you're in the room and someone's pitching you an idea that you don't immediately think is a good one, how is it that people have been able to change your mind?

Peter: They turn me by their credibility, and do I believe in them? I used to say frequently to the people who worked for me in those creative endeavors that if there is a good idea that

I turn down, and that the company doesn't make, it's your own fault. It's not my fault if I pass on a good idea; it's your fault that you've allowed me to pass on a good idea. And you need to do whatever it takes to convince me or the powers that be. If there's an idea that you really believe in, you need to do whatever it takes to get us to do it.

Suneel: Who's someone that stood up to you because they believed so strongly in their idea?

Peter: Let me tell you about *The X-Files*. I didn't get it at all. I thought it was one of the stupidest ideas I had ever heard. Bob Greenblatt, head of drama at the network at that point, is someone who had enormous credibility, someone I really believed in; he wasn't somebody who just believed in everything, and he kept arguing with me and kept saying, "Look, I think you're wrong, here's why I think you're wrong."

Look, I think what you try and do in those jobs is you try and set up a system of advocacy and you want to have people who really believe in their ideas, who are willing to fight for them and are willing to consider your positions on them. And are willing to give up on the ones where you're smarter, where you make points that they can't.

All of these things are fundamentally subjective. You're making bets. So there's no objective criteria, and that's frankly true of most entrepreneurial companies. Because by definition it doesn't exist, so you're looking to set up a system that tests two things. You're looking to set up a system that tests how thoughtful someone is: Have they really thought it through? Can they answer your objections? Are they open to your objections? Are they interested in hearing them? And then you want to test their passion. Do they really believe in it? Are they really willing to fight for it? Those strike me as the two best things you can look for.

Suneel: How do you test somebody's passion?

Peter: You tell them, "That's the stupidest idea I've ever heard," and see how they respond. You want to create environments where they are supportive of one another, but very direct with one another.

Nobody's right about everything. What you want is thoughtful people who will take input in, fight for those things they believe in, try to convince you why they believe in it, keep fighting for it, keep pushing for it. And then those things they don't believe in, or that they can't stand up for, have them say, "You know what, maybe you're right. Maybe I should give up on this."

Suneel: Is that what happened with *X-Files?*

Peter: Bob Greenblatt was capable of ordering scripts without my approval. He told me that he was ordering scripts. I go, "That's a stupid idea, but go for it." And when the script came in I read the script and said, "This is ridiculous. I don't get it at all." We argued about it, and he was more passionate about it than I was. I believed enormously in him; I thought he was one of the smartest young people I knew. I finally said, "Look, if you believe in it so much, go make the pilot." You're not committing to a whole series; you're committing to the first episode.

And then by the time the pilot came in, I still didn't get it. And everybody loved it, so at that point you should be both open-minded and curious enough to go, "Wow, there's something here because everybody else seems to love this and I'm obviously wrong about this and we should put it on the air."

The more people who were exposed to it, it was clear that he was right and I was wrong. That's exactly the system I wanted to set up.

Suneel: One of the things we keep coming back to is the importance of conviction. But the ideas you're betting on are brand-new. How do you build authentic conviction when there's not a lot of evidence out there that your idea will work?

Peter: A combination of two wildly disparate things. On the one hand, your conviction should be wholly analytical. It should be you've gone through the business plan, you've really thought hard about the marketplace, you have genuine curiosity about the marketplace. There's a whole series of exercises that are analytical.

And then there's a whole other set of things which are exactly the opposite, which are essentially gut. I'm looking to be moved, I'm looking to be excited, I'm looking for emotional, I'm looking for things that are cool, and I just think this is the coolest thing I ever heard, and listening to that gut. If you go, "Hey, look, I've done all this analysis of why I think this is a backable idea, but at the end of the day I fucking love it. I think this is so cool. I think this is exciting."

Suneel: You said that one of the things that we underestimate is how scary it is to be creative, because you're putting so much of yourself out there. What advice do you have for young people who want to be entrepreneurs or leaders inside bigger organizations?

Peter: I gave a talk at the Harvard Business School this year, and what I said to them is, "Look, unfortunately you've really been trained your whole life to do two things. Be obedient and to please adults."

That's fundamentally what our education system is about right now.

You better be really obedient and do what the teacher tells you to, and bring your homework in on time and study hard for tests, and figure out how to please a bunch of adults in authority. Success in the real world is the opposite—it's about being disruptive, it's about being bold, it's about being willing to fight for what you believe in. Being disruptive is the opposite of being obedient. And you can have a perfectly good little life if you've gone to Harvard Business School or one of these places, but you're not going to be the giant huge home run that you really want to be. Figure out how to really fight for what you believe in. Be willing to be disruptive, be willing to have unpopular ideas, be willing to take huge risks, and those are things that I think kids in college really need to start thinking about.

I think it's a real challenge for our educational system. I think the things we are pushing these kids to do from the time they're seven or eight years old until they are out of high school and into college are not necessarily the most valuable tools. The most valuable tools are thinking differently, being disruptive, taking big risks, being bold, being imaginative.

Suneel: Yeah, maybe that's your book, Peter.

Peter: Hey, the head of a business school told me I should write that as a book. I had the same response.

ADAM LOWRY, ENTREPRENEUR

Adam co-founded Method, the designer cleaning products company, which he later sold to SC Johnson. Recently, he co-founded Ripple Foods, which creates plant-based alternatives to dairy. Adam was one of the first people to drive home the importance of making your idea feel inevitable. What's happening in the world, and how does your idea fit in? And just like so many others, the origin story of Method was much different than the ending.

> "Raising money was really hard for Method because of the sector, the availability of cash, the fact that we were coming off of a pretty bad recession. Consumer products were totally out of vogue. But we scratched and clawed. And eventually we were able to, through lots of little nickels and dimes, get the capital that the business needed."

Carlye: What made Method different? What made the idea backable?

Adam: We created Method around this idea of design and sustainability coming together. We were really talking about the lifestyling of the home. We had identified that there was a big disconnect between the care that people were bringing to their homes—the amount of effort and thought that was going into how we curated our spaces culturally—there was a really big disconnect between that and the cleaning product world, which was all about nuclear toxic chemicals that you need to hide from your children so that they don't poison them.

We talked about making the cleaning product a home accessory. Something that could live out on the countertop and become part of your home. A dish soap sits on your countertop twenty-three hours and forty-five minutes every day and you use it for fifteen minutes. It should be something that works with your home.

Carlye: So, designer cleaning products? What showed you—and backers—that was inevitable?

Adam: It's a little bit hard to imagine because it's so frickin' long ago, but at the time, brands like Restoration Hardware, Pottery Barn, Williams-Sonoma, were really hitting their stride. You were starting to see the specialization of—I'll use the term "design," but it was basically like curating premium quality spaces within your living space.

We were seeing consumer momentum behind these things. It happened to be coinciding with a recession. Two thousand was when the dot-com bubble burst, and there was a short-term turn toward nesting. People saying, "Okay, well, the economy's not as good. I'm not going to eat out as much, but I'm going to pamper myself a little bit with items for my home and in my home." There were sort of both long-term cultural changes toward this sort of lifestyling of the home as well as the short-term economic pushes.

You were also starting to see it pop up in media. You had the *Real Simple*s of the world that were starting to essentially create a category about home. Those were all sorts of cultural indicators that something here was really changing in consumer mindsets.

Carlye: You identified this shift under way. How did you describe it to an investor?

Adam: We talked about it as the lifestyling of the home. We had a brand book that we used really early on, even before we really had a business pitch. It was really just sort of crystallizing this idea of a lifestyle brand within the cleaning space, which was a radical idea. People are like, "What the hell are you doing? Cleaning is about power and strength and bright-colored packaging type of thing." We were bringing this idea of a softer, more lifestyle type of approach.

Suneel: This is the first time I've heard of a brand book used to pitch an investor. What makes a good brand book and what was inside yours?

Adam: Think of a brand style guide on steroids. It basically articulated these macro trends that were going on. It was our hypothesis that this was a segment that was going to develop. It was very consumer oriented, from a consumer lens. Here is this sort of psychographic and cultural underpinning of these trends that we're seeing. Our hypothesis is that this creates opportunity within the home-care space because there's a progression. It's your home itself, the things you put in it, around you, the things you put on your body in the beauty space. And we were drawing these, saying, "Hey, the next logical step here is the cleaning space."

Then we articulated a brand. A lot of it was also then saying, "And the brand that you need to have here is going to be very different from Kaboom. It's going to be one that's not about power and strength and split-screen television commercials with three squirts versus four. It's going to be a very different brand proposition." And we articulated the Method brand, coming from the brand name itself, is really about technique rather than power, which was sort of an initial brand idea and using sustainable chemistries, green chemistries, to get the job done in a way that isn't poisonous, isn't toxic, works with your home, is safe on surfaces—the things in the sort of short term that people were really concerned about.

Carlye: A lot of people would go straight to the competitive landscape and differentiation. Why start with the macro trends?

Adam: For a lot of entrepreneurs, it was all about the product and then what's the strategy that we're going to try to turn this into a business? We did the opposite. We started with a realization that something was going to change and that there was a big opportunity. We were never going to win if we were just going to churn through more units than Tide.

Carlye: It sounds like you led with design, not sustainability, when you pitched your idea. Why?

Adam: In the early days, we almost had to kind of hide the sustainability part of it just because of the sort of business climate and culture at the time. The green cleaning segment, these sort of earthy, crunchy brands, was a very small segment at the time. Not a big enough one where if you positioned it like, "Hey, we're going to reinvent green cleaning," that it would be really interesting to investors. Ninety-six percent of people don't buy green cleaners. Our desire was to target them with a product that happens to be sustainably designed.

Carlye: Was it hard for you to make that decision to shelve the sustainability aspect of your brand? That's something that's important to you.

Adam: No, no, no. It wasn't hard. That decision was both strategic as well as philosophical. And this is a personal philosophy. I do not think sustainability should be a marketing positioning. Sustainability, all it is, is an aspect of the quality of a product and the quality of a company that makes those products and nothing else. It's either you have it and you have it to a greater degree or you don't.

If we're moving from a world where most things are not designed sustainably to a world where everything's going to be designed sustainably, it's not a differentiated position to say, "Hey, we're the green one." We never put a green leaf on the front of the package and called it Eco Planet. Because when everybody's eco planet, what are you? So, for me, it's very important that the sustainability of a product is just an aspect of the quality of the product. And we put the onus on ourselves to do that as best we can and better than any other brand.

Suneel: Can you take us back to the early days when you were raising your very first round of funding?

Adam: In late 2001, we basically had a paper route of twenty stores because nobody within the traditional sort of vendor source supply chain would talk to us. We were two guys making cleaning products in San Francisco. We were running out of money. We had $16 in the bank at one point and we had $300,000 in payables to our vendors. We weren't paying our vendors, so they said, "All right, we're not going to make any more product for you."

Raising money was really hard for Method because of the sector, the availability of cash, the fact that we were coming off of a pretty bad recession. Consumer products were totally out of vogue. But we scratched and clawed. And eventually we were able to, through lots of little nickels and dimes, get the capital that the business needed.

Suneel: In many ways that skepticism makes sense. You were two guys in your twenties without much of a track record. How did you convince them?

Adam: It's a combination of factors. We were in stores, we were selling through. A lot of it was just a lot of conversations—you're essentially being interviewed for things like your level of sort of passion and commitment as well as your skill set. And I was a frickin' climate scientist before I started this. How is that relevant? Part of it was convincing them that an outside perspective was actually an asset, not a liability, to execute this type of strategy. The reality is that the big companies are generally super blind to this type of innovation because they think of things through unmet-needs segments. And this would never show up as an unmet need. Understanding that an outsider perspective and the strategic approach that we were taking was actually not a liability but a necessity for executing something that was truly differentiated relative to Lysol and Windex and Fantastic.

Carlye: You recently started a new company, Ripple, a plant-based milk. How did you get people to get behind that idea?

Adam: It's inevitable that people are moving to much more plant-based diets. And it's mostly people that aren't exclusively plant-based. It's not all vegans and vegetarians, but it's people that are flexitarians and those people are not going to want to sacrifice nutrition and taste for that choice.

And so, our pitch is very much with Ripple Foods that the world is going plant based and if we're going to capture the opportunity that comes from that, the environmental opportunity, the human health opportunity, the business opportunity of that, the products have got to be as great as dairy is from a taste and nutrition standpoint. That's what we've based the Ripple business around.

Suneel: How do you convince people you are onto something real?

Adam: From a brand standpoint there was an analogy here to the cleaning space. When we entered the cleaning space, every brand was very problem-solution focused. Windex was about streak-free glass, right? It wasn't about a lifestyle. Pretty much every other brand in our space is focused on an ingredient. Almond Breeze is the brand name, Oatly. But ingredients go in and out of fashion. So if you base your brand around an ingredient that's not, in my opinion, a very enduring brand proposition. What does Almond Breeze do when almonds are going out of fashion, which they are right now?

What you actually want to do is you want to create a brand around what matters within the space. With the Ripple brand, there's no ingredients in the brand name and we don't talk about the ingredient as the reason to buy the product. We wanted to build a more enduring proposition—to solve for where this category is going for the long term. You start a business that's not a three-to-five-year thing. It's a long-term commitment.

TINA SHARKEY, ADVISOR, INVESTOR, AND ENTREPRENEUR

Tina is the co-founder of iVillage and Brandless. She served as the global chair and group president of BabyCenter and led multiple business units inside AOL. She is also the former president of the Sesame Workshop's Digital Group and currently serves on the board of directors for PBS and IPSY. She's seen backable traits succeed inside both big companies and startups—and her key takeaways are the same. She's the one who coined the term "armchair anthropologist" for us.

> "Deep empathy is a really critical factor. It's empathy, not just observation. Observation is just data, but empathy, really, is walking the walk with others and understanding not just pain points, but how they are living their lives."

Suneel: Most backers I talk to say they're looking for a sense of conviction. What does conviction mean to you? And, does someone have to convince themselves first?

Tina: I think the idea of conviction is 100 percent true and that backers of any sort, voters, leaders, all need to see that in the person that they are going to back. This idea of convincing yourself first is almost like the journey of conviction—how did you arrive at this? What insight led to your desire to go and do this thing, climb this hill, try and solve this problem, build a better mousetrap, fix an office system, fix whatever it is that you want to go do, build, or manifest?

Suneel: How do you get a sense of that? What do you look for?

Tina: I look for experience in the space, either personal or professional. Also, a deep passion to solve the problem for the community they're building it to serve. And then, a very convincing fact-based argument on why this problem or opportunity needs to be solved and why they are the right people and team. Finally, why now, why hasn't it been done before?

Suneel: This is the tough thing about new people and new ideas because on the one hand, it's unproven people who have new ideas that end up changing the world. But on the other hand, it seems like that's also the toughest thing to take a bet on because they're unproven and because new ideas are inherently risky.

Tina: They don't necessarily need to be proven. They don't have to have done it before. You need to be convinced that they have what it takes. They see something that others don't see, and they possess something that others don't possess. You need to believe that they're the people to go solve a problem that others haven't been able to solve, or build a better mousetrap.

Suneel: You mentioned this "journey of conviction." What does that look like for you? You've worked on all these different projects and all these different situations.

Tina: I like to solve problems to make things easier and to identify big dynamic shifts in consumer behavior and societal norms. Even if that shift is ultimately deployed in enterprise, it's still about people's habits and evolving engagement and consumption models. People are people. I'm like an armchair cultural anthropologist. I love to study people and cultures and the different ways in which they live and how all of our habits across generations are changing—and how that ladders up to massive global market shifts on both the consumer and enterprise landscapes.

Suneel: Can you give an example of what you mean?

Tina: Look at the cereal market—gigantic market, global adoption, big public companies that make cereal, distribute cereal, and yet cereal is falling off a cliff. People aren't eating cereal anymore the way they were. And the cereal companies are doing everything they can to win you back. Part of the assumed reason is the ingredient palette—the sugar, and we know about gluten. But that's not the reason, in my opinion, why people aren't eating cereal. The reason why people aren't eating cereal is because we were acculturated to cereal being a morning food. Right? Get out your bowl, pour the cereal, pour the milk, have a spoon, and you sit, and you have it as you read the back of the box. You may even have memories as a child reading the back of a cereal box. But today, people are eating breakfast with one hand because they're on their phone. They're likely not even pouring milk, or putting anything in a bowl, or sitting at a table. They're likely on their phone and they really only have one hand free and they want to get out the door.

When I get conviction, I have to not only see why I think this opportunity—this solution, product, service, fill in the blank—needs to exist in the world, but also why now? What are we seeing about the people who are ready to embrace this change? What about the ones who have already made a change and no one has caught up with them? I have to get conviction, not just that the product can be created and it's better, but that there's mass adoption waiting and that people want it.

Suneel: So it seems like if we're looking at the two ingredients of real belief here—it's belief in the mass adoption and it's also belief in the product. In some cases, the product might be clever, but there's no evidence that we're seeing a trend that people are ready for it. What would people have to show you? What would be the killer slide to convince you that this is inevitable?

Tina: I would want to see real data that the product market had shifted and that there was a behavior change that left a major gaping hole, which needed to be filled.

Suneel: Okay, so how about an example of a company that was built on inevitable behavior change?

Tina: Rent the Runway. I think one of the major impetuses for Rent the Runway is social media. You ask, "Wait, what does that have to do with renting dresses?" But it has everything to do with renting dresses if you understand the psychology behind the fact that people who are very social need something to talk about. They want to be in pictures all the time. That's the social currency. They're not even necessarily writing words. Outfits and outfit changes become the talking points. And you don't want to be seen in the same thing over and over again. It's not just the fact that you couldn't afford that gown, which is maybe how Jenn started the company, but now their biggest growth area is not gowns but everyday clothes. Yes, this offering checks the box of the sustainable closet—you don't want to buy things you're only going to wear a couple of times—but why people care that their outfits are always changing is because of social media. Social media would be a critical insight as to what is driving the behavior change.

Suneel: Really interesting. How do you coach people to come up with backable ideas?

Tina: When I'm creating ideas or working with founders or teams I often say, "Get in a helicopter above the problem or opportunity and observe what else is changing that might feel orthogonal to the idea but could play a big role in accelerating or derailing your idea."

In the case of something like rental clothing, it is not just about people having smaller closets, not wanting to buy things that they're not going to wear a lot, or not being able to afford the things they want. It is also about the fact that they don't want to be photographed twice in the same outfit because of their social media feeds. And it is also because people deeply care about the impact of overproduction and overconsumption and consumerism on climate change. They want to play a role in the sustainability movement. Re-commerce and rental clothing allows them to be part of the solution.

Suneel: It seems that every pitch requires two essential ingredients. How would you describe these two different things?

Tina: The insight and the behavior shift that follows. People eating breakfast with one hand is a non-obvious thing. It's a design-thinking approach to not only the product we want to sell but what environment we are selling that product into and what else we need to know about the market and the dynamic shift in consumption habits. I have always appreciated home ethnographic studies because what people tell you in a focus group is often not how they are actually living their lives. When you observe people in their homes and offices and see how they're actually living their lives, that's when the "aha moments" show up.

Suneel: In our research, we've heard a lot about the importance of practicing the pitch—and how to get genuine feedback. You don't just want to have someone tell you, "It's a great idea."

Tina: I really want to hear the objection. The why behind the "no." I don't want my pitch to be so rehearsed and polished that I didn't leave room to actually hear what the objections are. I can learn more from the objections than people saying, "Love it. Great. Wonderful." The accolades are easy. But if you have the privilege to meet with people who in some way, shape, or form have had an experience with other businesses or services, listen. It doesn't mean that you change your idea for the people in the room. It doesn't mean that you have to agree with everything they're saying or have an answer to everything. Just listen to their question and then ask them why they ask. People who are super studied and super practiced just want to perform their idea. And I think if you perform your idea, you're not really listening.

Suneel: You've mentioned this before. Active listening is a key part of pitching.

Tina: Yes, and it doesn't mean you have to have the answers. But I think you should write the questions down, and then debrief with yourself or your team. You don't have to address all of the questions or objections, but make sure you understand them because there are a lot of gems in there that you would be well served to pay attention to. Again, it doesn't mean that just because somebody has a question or someone has a negative piece of feedback that that's the right thing. But often there's a lot that's really helpful there, which people just leave on the table. It's such gold.

Suneel: That's the first time I've heard that insight very tactically. I should be writing down everything that's coming up—questions, objections—so that I see the patterns?

Tina: Yes. And also, really pay attention to body language because it's really important in the early part of your pitch, before you sell your idea, that you get everybody on the same page. Start with creating that connection by creating a shared data set that everybody can agree on before you actually sell your idea. People who do this well do it naturally.

You talk about selling personal nutrition training; everybody wants it. But you share that people think it's too expensive. They can't find someone who they can work with, or who works with their schedule. And what you're doing in that moment where you are describing that is creating a connection with people in the room. Everyone is starting from a place of agreeing with each other.

Suneel: This seems like a useful practice in just about any room.

Tina: There's incontrovertible facts, right? Any good politician uses this. Everybody wants to pay less taxes; everybody wants affordable healthcare. You start with the things that are universal wants and desires before you get to the problems you're solving.

We talked about Rent the Runway; by using that example, I got you to agree with me that the target audience is on Instagram, they're posting this many photos. Snapchat is a visual thing. Smartphones are enabling all of this. Photography is a new lingua franca. Those have nothing to do with gowns. But we were both agreeing that that was the state of the world—and then by the time we got into the gown piece, I already had you agreeing with me. It wasn't a manipulation because it was just stating an observation. When we were talking about cereal I started with how people are reading their phones in the morning, whether it's email or the news, which means their hand is busy. And you agreed with me because it's true. That's a way to get the people on the other side of the table to be on the same side as you. They may not agree with the idea because you haven't told them the idea yet, but you're all agreeing on the facts and observations that led you there.

Suneel: Do you see a relationship between universal truth and the behavior observations we were talking about earlier?

Tina: I think that you start with universal truth. I'm making these numbers up—95 percent of American homes have mobile phones. That's just a universal truth. Then the observation is: People are on them X number of hours a day. Those are just facts. Before you ever got to the insight around the fact that they're eating breakfast with one hand, you're just starting with the fact, the universal truth. It creates instant connection where everyone is dealing with and working off the same data.

Suneel: Okay. And so then I might say 95 percent of households have mobile phones; people are on their device three hours a day. People around the room are nodding. Then I can evolve into a behavioral insight as a result.

Tina: You can talk about the typical day from 1950, 1970, 1990, 2000, 2010, 2020, and that could be one slide with a little icon of a family. You see the nuclear family with everyone having breakfast, sitting at the table together. Mom is wearing an apron, Dad's drinking a cup of coffee, kids are nicely eating their cereal, all behaved, all perfect—that's maybe 1950s. And then today: kids are eating alone, the parents have two jobs, the nuclear family is a myth. Everyone's with you as you explain this. And then you can go into the behavior change of why you really want to take on the breakfast-bar market. And if someone wonders, "Wait, why are you talking about the shifting family behavior?" Well, it's clear: breakfast is a mainstay of the American diet. And look how breakfast has changed. And so, if we're going to make a new snack bar or whatever, we're going to make it a breakfast bar because we have established that there's room and reason that bars are the new cereal.

Suneel: It's fascinating because if somebody was creating a pitch deck for a cereal bar, they probably wouldn't spend the first couple of slides talking about mobile phones.

Tina: Probably not most people. A lot of times, people tell me I have too many slides until they see how quickly I go through them. I never base myself on the number of slides, because it's more like they are just an illustration to get people on the same page. Setting up those universal truths and setting up the insights are a great way to get to the place where we can talk about "Why?" That's the why now, and what's changed. And then you have to go to the "Why us?" and "Why now?"

ANDY DUNN, FOUNDER

Andy is the co-founder and former CEO of Bonobos. In 2017, he sold the company to Walmart for more than $300 million. What became clear during our conversation is how Bonobos helped pave the way for other companies, like Warby Parker, Allbirds, and Away, to build internet-driven brands. Dunn and his co-founder, Brian Spaly, were seen as one of the first startups to take this on, when many investors doubted it could be done.

> "It's not really worth talking about what's going to happen in years three to five, because you got to go do years one and two anyway...Let's not spend too much time talking about a future that we have to earn the right to."

Carlye: We understand that you knew your first backer, Joel Peterson, from an idea you were chasing before Bonobos—one that didn't work. Is that right?

Andy: Joel tells a story in a funny way, which is that I had chosen him as an adviser for a project I was working on in a class at Stanford. It was to import this premium beef jerky from South Africa called biltong. It's this really high-quality beef that the African folks developed in the seventeenth century; they would cure meat with salt, pepper, olive oil, coriander, and then cook it in these wooden boxes with a little see-through panel, and it would be cured by the sun.

I spent some time looking at it and we found the market was there; the taste tests were really good. There was just one small problem, which is that it is illegal to serve uncooked meat in the U.S. We got to the end of the project and I told Joel, "Hey, I don't think we can do this; here's why." I later found out that he was pleased that even though we'd put all this energy into it, I was willing to walk away from it.

Carlye: So, what happened when you approached him with your next endeavor?

Andy: I came to Joel and pitched him on the idea of taking these better-fitting pants my co-founder had developed and building an internet-driven model where we'd go direct to the consumer. I said we were emulating some of what we were seeing from third-party marketplace e-commerce disrupters at the time, like Zappos, with free shipping both ways and free returns within 365 days of purchase. And basically said we were going to be the pioneer in how these next-generation brands get built by going DTC, direct to consumer, over the internet.

I spent the meeting just sharing the idea, asking Joel for feedback as we went. And we got to the end of the meeting and he synthesized and said, "This reminds me of my first meeting with David Neeleman from JetBlue. We're going to go into a stagnant industry with a really customer-centric approach. We're going to cut out the middle person." He was instantly speaking about it in terms of "we," which was really exciting.

Later, the way Joel told the story, the decision to walk away from the beef jerky idea really informed him feeling like I was someone that he could back. The ability to have walked away from another idea gave him confidence when we started walking toward that Bonobos idea.

Suneel: This ability to walk away and having that be a signal for backers—that's really interesting. We haven't heard that before.

Andy: It's like the conventional wisdom is wrong. "Don't ever quit" is the wrong motto—it's "Don't ever quit unless you should quit." Can you endure the things that you shouldn't quit doing? That's the question. Like, people that give up on anything are not backable, but people who are unwilling to quit on certain things are also not backable.

Suneel: If I'm looking at your story, it's as if walking away from the beef jerky idea and walking toward Bonobos showed an investor like Joel that you had conviction. It gave him faith in your diligence.

Andy: Exactly. At Bonobos, we always talked about the five human traits. We called them our core virtues: self-awareness, empathy, positive energy, judgment, and intellectual honesty. Intellectual honesty really is a way of saying, are you data driven and do you have the courage to change your mind? There's something surprising about people, which is that we have a hard time divorcing ourselves from historical positions that we've held. This is something human beings are not good at.

There's a really good organizational behavior psychology experiment, the Green Triangle case, where three different groups of people are given different sets of data about the

Challenger disaster. I was the only person in a class at Stanford Business School in my OB [organizational behavior] class that actually moved from one group to the other—when pretty much everyone should move when they give you this intervening data set. It seems like a small thing, but sadly the willingness to change one's mind in the face of new data is unusual.

Back to Joel. He also knew that I turned down an offer at a venture capital firm, a job that was hard to get, and that might also have created more conviction. He didn't know the specifics and numbers, but I had barely enough money to pay rent. And then $160,000-plus of debt from business school. Having someone who's willing to jump in and take a risk when the circumstances would dictate that it's irrational is a very magnetizing thing for backing someone.

Carlye: You started with pants but today you have an entire menswear line. Did you share that vision early on?

Andy: After Joel committed to investing, I pitched Andy Rachleff, who was another storied lecturer at Stanford and co-founder of Benchmark Capital—and someone who I also really admire. And at the back of the deck there was a slide that talked about how we were going to focus on pants for a few years and then we were going to build this full menswear offering. I think we showed shirts, suits, accessories, and then we even had personal care, painting this ten-year or eight-year vision of how we would expand. And I remember Andy saying, "I don't even want you to think about shirts until you've shown excellence in pants." There may have even been a conversation around something like "You got to be at a 10 million run rate in your first product before you think about the second."

I watched other founders—when I became an angel investor—try to move to product 2 too quickly. My learning from Bonobos was, until you've gotten product 1 right, no one's going to care about product 2. And so it was this duality of we're going to focus on selling a lot of pants out of the gate. But the vision here is in terms of the Bonobos brand to build something that can (1) be a true multicategory men's apparel brand, and (2) prove that business model disruption, internet first, is going to be core to building brands going forward.

Carlye: Do you find any tension in presenting the immediate focus and the long-term big vision?

Andy: That mixture of near-term focus and big vision actually is a tension that, depending on the moment, could be helpful or harmful to our company. Five years later I started to see a whole ecosystem of brands emerging. "Let's build a multi-brand platform that can support it," I said, and went out and pitched a bunch of investors. I can actually remember being in a pitch meeting at Andreessen Horowitz where I pitched the Bonobos story and then this vision of where we could take it. And later I found out that that second component of the meeting killed their interest in investing because they felt like I wasn't focused.

Suneel: But future vision does excite people. When you were first meeting with Joel, you talked about wanting to be the pioneer in how these next-generation brands get built. How did you make a leap from selling better-fitting pants out of a duffel bag to saying "We want to pioneer how next-generation brands get built"?

Andy: It was really a past is predictor of the future, which is if you want to see the future, look to the past. I had been fortunate to work in 2002 for Lands' End as a Bain consultant and saw the power of this direct-to-consumer catalog company to go to the customer and build a great relationship.

I remember walking in to the Lands' End call center—this is pre-email—and I read a note on the wall that said, "Dear Elizabeth, Thank you so much for waking me up the morning of my wedding. My bridesmaids wanted to sleep in. My mom was a wreck. I'm so grateful to you for giving me a call. Sincerely, Catherine." And I remember thinking, "Whoa, this is crazy. The relationship between this Lands' End call-center rep and this customer." And so here I am in 2007 at Stanford Business School, the internet is going crazy, the consumer internet is in the very early days, Facebook was three years old, Twitter was a year old, Instagram hadn't even been invented yet...and it just clicked for me. I was like, wait, the internet should be a better catalog; it should be more personalizable; you're not limited by the number of pages.

Carlye: And that is what happened, right?

Andy: In 2009 these Wharton students came into our offices saying they were going to build a Bonobos-type model in eyewear. And I remember thinking, "Wait, eyewear is going to be really hard." But we got excited about it; my co-founder made an angel investment; I later became an angel investor in Warby Parker. And from there, we've seen this whole direct-to-consumer evolution flower and it's been really fun to be a part of it. As an angel investor in companies like Away and Glossier and Harry's and Warby, I really feel like we've gotten a front-row seat at how this internet-driven DTC innovation has flowered and I think will ultimately move into every corner of the consumer retail ecosystem. It already is.

Suneel: In some ways this is exactly what you talked to Joel about in that first meeting.

Andy: I remember when Bonobos got to about $100,000 of monthly sales, six months after we launched, I woke up at three in the morning in my bedroom. I was sleeping in a stockroom. We had four hundred pairs of pants in inventory, which I kept in my bedroom; we were doing pick, pack, and ship out of our house—which is not good for work-life balance, by the way. And I woke up at three in the morning and I thought, "Holy shit, I'm sitting on a secret. I'm sleeping in the stockroom of this internet-driven pants retailer and one day everything in the world of brand building is going to have these digitally centric models. And digitally centric upstarts are going to disrupt virtually every category. And no one believes me." At this time I would meet people in New York in the fashion industry and they'd be like, "Where do you sell?" The answer typically was, "Well, I sell at Barneys or Bloomingdale's," and I'd be like, "Just online." And the looks of pity in people's eyes, like, "What a loser, he has no distribution."

Suneel: You're investing and advising other early-stage founders now.

Andy: Yes, I've made a few dozen angel investments in 2020. An example: I met a founder recently who's got a really cool nontoxic cookware company called Caraway. It's very relevant to a movie I saw last year with my parents called *Dark Waters*, which is about how DuPont manufactured this pretty corrosive

Teflon substance that ended up poisoning a lot of people. So, chemical-free dishware is actually a pretty interesting concept, and it's really taking off through COVID. I just liked this entrepreneur. He's tenacious and will be successful. But some investors say it's too small of a category.

Suneel: Is it possible that this tenacious founder doing the chemical-free cookware company could tie that to a bigger vision? Is it possible that cookware is just the tip of the iceberg and that if you get that right, it'd lead to something bigger? Would backers want to hear about that?

Andy: Totally. Yeah. You could build the next-generation Williams-Sonoma starting in cookware, right? You have to see around corners when backing people. You want people focused on nailing product 1, but who have vision for products 2, 3, and 4. Cookware is probably one of the core hero products of a brand like that. But many venture investors don't always have the ability to see which entrepreneurs are going to be good at discontinuous innovation over time. It's not easy. It's hard to know who can do that.

Carlye: Do you ever have two narratives? Things that are in the back of your head that you hold inside, and other things that you would share with a backer?

Andy: There is an idea that a friend and I have for something new called Pumpkin Pie, and one of the things that's exciting about it is that we can self-fund it out of the gates. He's an entrepreneur and has also been fortunate to have had a bit of success with his two companies. Bootstrapping—you just don't have to deal with that tension because investors are idiosyncratic and people may not agree with the vision, and at the end of the day there's no way to resolve it other than through actually doing the startup.

And the truth is it's not really worth talking about what's going to happen in years three to five, because you got to go do years one and two anyway. And so debates about what isn't in the near term can be unproductive. Establishing that there is a view of it is helpful, but it's not worth talking about. I was talking to one of my friends yesterday about this new concept and we kind of bantered about where it could go, and then at some point we said, it actually doesn't matter yet. Let's just be focused. Let's just be focused on what the MVP is. Let's not spend too much time talking about a future that we have to earn the right to.

BRIAN GRAZER, PRODUCER

Brian co-founded Imagine Entertainment with Ron Howard. His films and television shows have been nominated for more than 40 Academy Awards and more than 190 Emmys. Before our meeting began, we sat in his lobby, surrounded by people preparing to pitch Grazer. I hadn't been nervous up until that point. But the conversation with Grazer was easy, maybe because making ideas backable is what he lives and breathes.

> "People don't really like numbers. Numbers are very important, but they don't remember numbers. Numbers don't reach your heart. When you reach somebody's heart, that moves them to do things or to not do something."

Suneel: You've said that you really enjoy the process of "case building" a brand-new idea. What is case building?

Brian: I would look at case building like this. I look at everything as a story. All those tech guys—I speak to them and their friends, whether it's Brian Chesky, Jack Dorsey, Tim Cook, or Satya Nadella—they look at their business as a story and they try to keep it simple, and they sometimes modify their story if they feel it needs to be modified. But there's a "why." *Why does this even exist?* And that's what I do with movies. You can pick any one of my movies and I'll case build it for you a little bit. Let's take *Apollo 13*.

Suneel: Sure.

Brian: *Apollo 13* started with a twelve-page outline that Jim Lovell got to me. But I didn't really know who Jim Lovell was. I didn't really know very much about aerospace, or the Apollo missions or anything like that. I read it and could see that there are multiple elements in these twelve pages. *Apollo 13* could have been about space, going into space, aerospace, the hardware of going into space, all those things that involve aerodynamics. Or, it could be about survival. I know very little about aerospace, and that wasn't a vocabulary that I was excited about getting involved with to begin with, but the subject that interested me the most, that lived inside of what would become this movie, was resourcefulness—human resourcefulness, and survival.

There's a mythic element that turns you on cinematically or optically when you watch an astronaut getting ready for a launch. I thought to myself, "Aren't you scared?"

And that just fascinated me. I thought that was really interesting that these guys are trying to go into outer space, theoretically to propel themselves into outer space and sling-shot around the moon. That seemed really crazy.

Suneel: So at its heart, this was a film about survival.

Brian: I would wake up every day once I bought the twelve pages—that then became a manuscript that was then going to become a book—I would case build every day as to why it should even be, why should it even exist as a movie. And I had to have all of those answers as to why Universal Pictures is going to give me—I think in this case it was $65 million.

Why they're going to give me $65 million. And that is a constant assault into the heartbeat of the why. Why should this even exist? I found that survival is a universal theme. In this case, their survival is motivated by heroism, patriotism, doing something for the country.

Suneel: What I'm hearing is that when you're case building, what can be even more important than factors like the market or competition is the underlying theme.

Brian: Yes. Ultimately you want to set and embrace what you think is the theme of a movie. In *A Beautiful Mind* it was about love. In *Friday Night Lights* it was about self-respect. In the movie *8 Mile,* it was about self-respect. In the movie *Apollo 13* it was about finding resources inside of you as a human being that you never thought existed in order to survive. So, astronauts, they're a level 10 on the intellectual scale, and they're a level 10 physically, and they go into outer space and this thing happens. They have to say, how am I going to solve this? And that's where they had to figure out how to get the square peg in the round hole, because how do you continue to solve these problems to survive? In movies, the underlying theme is what makes these things relatable to human beings, not just relatable to these three guys that are astronauts in outer space.

Suneel: But what happens when you're sitting across from somebody who's thinking just about the numbers and trying to figure out the ROI [return on investment] on the $65 million?

Brian: I mostly address the ROI thematically as opposed to the story, because if you're doing it with the story, then you can get judged for punctuation, grammar, and whoever's giving you the money can say, "Well, that doesn't make sense." But love makes sense.

Suneel: Why does the theme of love feel like the right bet for a studio?

Brian: Because you know that everybody's destination, a human destination for all in the world, is to have the connective tissue to somebody, and love is that connective tissue. So you have to prove that that's demonstrated within the story that you're telling. In the case of *Apollo,* we had to prove out survival. Sometimes it's emotional survival. I mean, they could have broken down emotionally and therefore they wouldn't function, any one of those three astronauts.

The exterior skin of a movie is the story. The interior of the movie would be that heartbeat that I'm trying to sell an executive that's going to give me $65 million or $165 million. We can't prove it out literally. Because if you try to prove it out literally, you're going to get chopped right off. You have to have a dream, and then you have to really unify your dream to reality.

Suneel: How can we apply this principle of theme outside of Hollywood? You're involved with startups. What's an example of a startup theme?

Brian: In the case with Brian Chesky, with Airbnb, it might be community. They originally thought they were doing it for all the reasons that you know, but it was like creating a community where people got to know people because socialization is essential to life.

Suneel: If Brian Chesky were coming to you with the idea of Airbnb, so this is like eight years ago, and he said, "I need your help pitching the investors," what would you have told him?

Brian: Well, I did help him. I told him it's about story, story, story. People don't really like numbers. Numbers are very important, but they don't remember numbers. Numbers don't reach your heart. When you reach somebody's heart, that moves them to do things or to not do something.

Suneel: You have to lead with the story.

Brian: You have to lead with the story and what you're trying to accomplish with the story.

Suneel: You've heard thousands of pitches now. You've been on both sides of the table so many times, and you obviously have to say no so many more times than you have to say yes. Is there something that tends to work for you more times than not?

Brian: Originality. When someone is trying to build a case, if they generalize, I ding them out.

Suneel: What's an example of generalizing? With *Apollo 13*, could you have generalized and lost the pitch?

Brian: Generalizing would be saying that "everybody, human beings are interested in adventure. There's nothing more fascinating than adventure in space." But who could relate to that? That'd be kind of generalizing. We did this series called *Mars*, and I did it with Elon Musk. It's at National Geographic.

Suneel: Yeah. It's really good.

Brian: Oh, thanks. It was cinematically pretty good. But I wanted people in the world or whoever's going to potentially watch it to know *why* we're even trying to go to Mars. And I don't think we succeeded in answering that question. On *Apollo 13*, we did focus better because we cut away to the parents, and the kids, and the priest. Cutting away like that reminded us all of the human qualities that were involved. Even early on, it gauged us to believe there's bravery involved and sacrifice involved. I think they get the human dimension, which was what we were trying to do the most.

Suneel: In some ways it's like pairing this theme that's irrefutable, this theme that everybody understands, with the originality of an idea.

Brian: Yeah, the originality of an idea. I don't want to do an idea other people have done. That's why I do these curiosity conversations every week because I learn so much. It helps me curate original ideas. The gut, everyone thinks it's a gut, but you have to have an informed gut. I don't really respect people that just say it's my gut or it's my instinct. If it's informed, then I'd be more interested. I like when things are substantiated.

Suneel: Can you give me an example of this balance?

Brian: I pick cultures to investigate and make movies or television shows about. I did another on the Wu-Tang Clan. I don't know if it's going to be successful, but I know the Wu-Tang Clan isn't corny. Why do I know it? I've met so many people in the world of hip-hop. I'm constantly asking little kids and old-school guys, the OGs. I might ask Dre, and his vote is equal to my son Patrick, who's fourteen. You have to cross-check all this stuff. I can tell you one hundred rappers that I wouldn't do. And there's a reason I picked the Wu-Tang Clan. Do I feel like they've been overplayed? Do I feel like they've oversaturated themselves? Those answers have to be no, I don't feel that they've oversaturated. What is their story? They grew up in Staten Island. They were all in and out of prison, and they created a band that became really big. And became the progenitors of a style of music. So I like that.

Suneel: I watched a talk you gave and one of the audience members raised his hand and asked, "Hey, Brian, I've written my idea down. I put pen to paper. Now, how do I get it made?" Your response to him is you have got to talk about your idea in the sexiest, hookiest way possible. That was your advice to him. What's an example of an un-sexy, un-hooky way to describe a movie?

Brian: I want to make a movie about David Frost and Richard Nixon's conversation. That's not sexy.

Suneel: That's not sexy.

Brian: No. The sexy way is there was a conversation between David Frost and Richard Nixon that was as brutal a fight as any fight you'd see. It was a David and Goliath story.

Nixon was a really smart, aggressive bully. And this little talk show host with a British accent brought down the president of the United States.

Suneel: I have so many questions, but I know we only have a minute here. Imagine that somebody's standing outside this office right now. They're about to come here and they're about to pitch you. What advice can I give them to improve their odds?

Brian: "Did you know in Atlanta, Georgia, there was a high school that every single rapper came out of? Andre 3000, Big Boi came out of it. Every single rapper came out of this one high school in Atlanta, Georgia. Did you know that?" No, I didn't know that. Tell me about it. And then it just goes like that.

Suneel: You're hooking them right away.

Brian: I want someone to say, "Did you know this happened? Did you know this existed?" And then ignite enough curiosity that I'll engage in the story.

ANN MIURA-KO, VENTURE CAPITALIST

Ann was the first professional investor to take a chance on my startup, Rise. When she decided to invest, others followed because of her reputation. She is the co-founder of Floodgate, which has invested in more than a hundred early-stage startups including Lyft, Chegg, and Twitch. Ann is a repeat member of the *Forbes* Midas List and the *New York Times* Top 20 Venture Capitalists Worldwide.

> "Different is oftentimes way more compelling than better. Because different sticks. Different is memorable. Different matters. Different isn't based on some other conception of something. If you have the chance, be different, not better."

Suneel: You were one of the earliest investors in Lyft—in fact, you backed them when they were called Zimride and not many were interested. What was it that made you decide to take a chance on them?

Ann: This is going to make me look a lot more prescient than I was because in that same time period we turned down Airbnb and Pinterest. There's a bunch of companies where we didn't see it. But what I liked about this company and these two founders was that transportation was a space where we didn't see startups at that time. Co-founders John and Logan did a very effective job of convincing us that this was a huge base that would have meaningful impact.

Suneel: How so?

Ann: If you look at their original pitch, they say that transportation itself has transformed the physical landscape of the United States multiple times, and that if we see another transportation revolution, it will have the same level of impact on the United States. That changes the way people live, it changes where they live, it changes their relationship between work and home life, it changes vacations—it changes a lot of different things.

Suneel: That's a big vision. One thing that keeps coming up is how important a big vision is to a compelling pitch. But how do you strike a balance between a big vision and a believable vision?

Ann: There is a very thin line between the visionary founder and the founder who is purely having visions. Look at stories like Theranos or that documentary on the Fyre Festival—those were visionary founders who just turned out to be having visions.

The difference between those kinds of founders and the founders that we're looking for are that the founders we want to back are creating that dotted line to what could be, but in the meantime they actually have a strong commitment themselves to making that dotted line. They're not just outsourcing that portion.

Suneel: How do you know that they're not outsourcing it? How do you know that they're for real?

Ann: They're very deeply involved in the experiments that lead there. They are deeply involved in finding the things that create the next step that gets us closer on that bottom line. Sometimes it's a new product; sometimes it's a new business model; sometimes it's a new pricing scheme. But it's not just sort of dancing at the edges—you're inside.

When I look at the way that Logan and John conducted themselves, not only were they selling this platform, but they were also recognizing what wasn't working, and then they were trying to figure out if it worked, what does it look like—and what does that mean?

They're trying to figure out how to make this whole thing come together fast, but it's not just about the speed; it's also about how to pull together all of the pieces that ultimately make it the compelling vision they imagined. As an example, they were thinking, If this all comes together, it will be a high-density situation and there will be lots of activity within the actual application. So, initially they were selling to universities, and then they thought, What if we connected all of these communities? Is there a way to connect one corporation with Stanford University, so you have Hewlett-Packard signed up, and Facebook? Then, would you actually have enough density to make this vision start to come true, of people sharing the rides often? Then when that didn't happen, then they were looking for other mechanisms, whether it was other kinds of long-distance rides between San Francisco and Los Angeles, or San Francisco and Lake Tahoe. Are there other ways of connecting these communities? You know that the founder is not just having visions when they're working on those intermediary experiments to get closer and closer to product market fit.

Suneel: You saw them actually digging in personally.

Ann: Yeah, Logan would actually drive vans between San Francisco and Los Angeles.

Suneel: Logan has been described as being a very mild-mannered person, an introvert. That's not the personality that most people think of when they think of somebody in this role. What is it about someone like Logan that makes him persuasive to you?

Ann: The magical thing that a leader has is storytelling. It's not a superpower granted only to extroverts. Storytelling is a power that is granted to almost anyone if they practice it. I know people who are severely dyslexic who are some of the most powerful storytellers. Quiet leaders, introverted leaders, can still have that power. I believe that Logan has that. Logan and John told a story. There's a hero; there is a nasty villain in cars that exist all over the place—most of them aren't being utilized, or when they are utilized there's only one person in the car. How do we make our roadways more efficient? How do we make them a better experience? Those types of questions and those types of stories really resonated with people.

Also, because they were great storytellers, they were able to be different, and they avoided mindless competition, especially in a very crowded and highly competitive field. And because they were effective storytellers, they could tell you Uber is your own personal driver, but Lyft is your friend who's coming to pick you up. That story was so different and so interesting. Different is oftentimes way more compelling than better. Because different sticks. Different is memorable. Different matters. Different isn't based on some other conception of something. If you have the chance, be different, not better.

Suneel: Storytelling can probably mean different things to different people. What are some of the ways that storytelling is done wrong?

Ann: Storytelling, when it's done wrong, is told as an analogy. We are like something else. We are Uber for X. What I want to hear about is, what is a horrible situation? What is a major wrong that's being inflicted upon the customer? Who is doing that to these customers, and why? And why won't they fix it? Why can't they fix it? And then who's a hero? Where do they come from? And why are they acting upon this problem?

You have to construct that kind of story that is purely based on your motivations, rather than, "Look at this great company that just made a ton of money, or is valued really high, now we're going to be just like it but a little bit better." It sets the context in a very different way, and it puts the investor or the employee or anyone else, the partners, into a different mindset.

Suneel: How do you convince yourself enough to convince the person on the other side of the table?

Ann: You have gut intuition, you have competitive data, you might have the product actually out of market, and you have data on that product, whether it's really early stage or more mature, and you have customer interviews. Some of it might be around complete lack of competition, and why is there lack of competition? Maybe there's industry dynamics that prevent a competitor from entering and you've just figured out how to circumvent that. Maybe you know that your customers are deeply unsatisfied with the current solutions for a certain set of reasons.

Or maybe something is actually changing. You have factories where certain data is now suddenly available and yet no one is taking advantage of that data. There are different reasons as to why I should now recognize that a change event has happened and so as a result of that, there's a huge new opportunity that's been created. Those kinds of earned secrets become the basis of the stories that I like to hear.

Suneel: Some of the companies that you invested in, even the ones that became wildly successful, like Lyft, struggled between the point that you wrote a check and the point when they raised their next round of funding. What's most important for someone who is going through the struggle?

Ann: Some of it is just persistence, and some of it is just this fighting instinct. Both John and Logan come across as very nice people. Back in 2011, when transportation was really heating up, people believed that you needed to be hyperaggressive in this type of market. So the question that we kept on getting from VCs was, "John and Logan, are they just too nice?"

There was some point at which I had talked to them and I had said, "You need to imagine that you drink tiger's blood, and go in there and show that side of you, because it exists." John and Logan managed to convince Raj Kapoor at Mayfield to invest shortly thereafter. And Logan in this email attaches a term sheet, and the only thing he wrote at the top was, "Tiger's blood attached."

Suneel: And now they're a public company.

Ann: Right before the IPO I wrote them a quick note of congratulations, and they said, "Thanks for believing. We might have acted like we had a ton of options back then, but really you were the only one." We've seen situations where we were the only believers, and they've gone wildly well. We've also seen situations where we were one of lots of people wanting to get into a round, and those companies didn't necessarily go well.

Especially at the early stage, just how excited everyone else is has nothing to do with how well that company will perform. Pinterest is a great example; in their seed round, basically everyone turned them down. It's really interesting to see how these companies transform over time and the humility you need to have as an investor to recognize you actually don't know. You don't know where it will go, and you're just investing in people and you're hoping that they can figure out a way to make it great.

Suneel: All things equal, do you feel like someone with a more brash personality tends to have a leg up in these early-stage pitches?

Ann: I don't think so. I think in a high-testosterone environment, probably that does register better. But I've never seen that as a fundamental competitive advantage. This is why I think having a more diverse investor set is probably a good thing.

People assume that being competitive is not compatible with being kind. Brad Smith, the former CEO of Intuit, says, "Never mistake kindness for weakness." One of the best CEOs in Silicon Valley says this, and I believe him. I believe that it's actually an incredible strength. You can build a great organization when it has that underlying set of values.

TREVOR MCFEDRIES, "YUNG SKEETER," RECORDING ARTIST, DJ, AND ENTREPRENEUR

When I first met Trevor, he had just raised $6 million from top investors for his new startup, Brud, which creates virtual celebrities for Instagram. But before becoming a tech entrepreneur, Trevor was known as Yung Skeeter, an artist who performed at music festivals like Lollapalooza and Coachella and produced, DJ'd, or directed for acts like Katy Perry, Azealia Banks, and Steve Aoki. In 2008, he was given the People's Choice Award for Best DJ by *Paper* magazine. We spoke about identity and the importance of not hiding who you truly are.

> "When I was a DJ in a past life, I used to walk into certain nightclubs, and there'd be a room full of dudes in New York Yankees hats. And I'd be like, 'Oh shit, I got to play some Jay-Z and New York rap music tonight.' But I actually had better success when I played the music that I knew really well. And that's what I tried to do later as an entrepreneur. Instead of trying to speak the language that felt like some Stanford MBA dude, I got to speak to it in the way that I know, because it will translate and it will connect."

Suneel: In our last conversation you told me about how top clubs would book you to play hip-hop, but you actually didn't like hip-hop music.

Trevor: Yeah. When I started making music and playing music, there wasn't really a dance-music scene in mainstream club culture. At the time it was like Lil Jon and rap music, especially for America. I was making house music, but I oftentimes would be booked in locations where you have a generation of people that only wanted to hear hip-hop. Initially I tried to be all things to all people and I would try to prepare sets that would allow me to play just hip-hop to hip-hop crowds. Because I didn't really know it that well, I think it felt kind of disingenuous.

Suneel: So you decided to change it up?

Trevor: What I tried to do instead is walk into a room, be myself, kind of beat them over the head with what I know and what I appreciate. It came together a bit more cohesively because it felt authentic and had a vibe, an authentic vibe. People would either get on board or they wouldn't, but people who got on board would appreciate something that felt different but also felt really exciting.

Suneel: When you first made that switch, what kind of a response did you get from the crowd?

Trevor: It would be pretty brutal. But I think what I tried to do instead was walk into spaces and not pretend to be something at the start and then kind of abruptly switch halfway through. I'd walk into a space and say, "This is who I am. Get on the train or get out." And I've recognized that people oftentimes—when they are approached with something that's different but that feels good—they'll go for the ride. And so

I would just walk into a room and be like, "All right, you're probably going to hate this for ten minutes, but then you're going to come around to it."

Suneel: What were some of the more memorable reactions?

Trevor: Oh, I mean, you can imagine everything. I remember playing in a club in Jersey that was a kind of a more mainstream spot, and I started playing house music, and this pretty buff, kind of like *Sopranos*-type character comes up to me and was like, "Look, I don't really like you. I don't believe in what you people are for. But you're playing this music, my girlfriend is loving it. I've never really met any gay people, but I like what you're doing." And he just assumed that because I was playing house music, I was a gay dude. It was this bizarre backhanded compliment. There have been other situations where people will come at you and offer you hundreds of dollars to stop.

Suneel: But as a DJ, isn't the goal to please the crowd?

Trevor: You can't be everything to everyone. When you try that it seems like the obvious solution, and you end up upsetting everybody because you're kind of half-assing all of the above. And so you end up being like, "Okay, I'm going to be the best version of myself and I'm going to try to make eye contact with the one person who's dancing and enjoying it," and being like, "Yeah, thank you. Get your other friends involved." And now there's a little pocket of them; you're looking at them and kind of egging them on. There's this understood commitment where I'll keep playing a record you like if you keep the dance floor going. If enough people are enjoying themselves, maybe others will get on board.

Suneel: When you started playing the music you wanted to play, did new opportunities begin to emerge?

Trevor: Absolutely. I definitely started making headway in that I was being who I was. I think if I just played the kind of music everyone was hearing day in, day out, you're not really differentiated. But you walk into a space and you're playing house music, all of a sudden at the end of the night you have some person who's like, "Man, I went to Israel for a summer and I heard all this music that sounded like this and I loved it...I'm a VP at Warner Bros. and I would love to get you to play our holiday party," or something like that. And all of a sudden, you're finding your tribe. Instead of just being another glossy box of cereal in the cereal aisle, all of a sudden you're the gluten-free granola. And if you're gluten-free, people that are gluten-free are going to be excited about it and tell their friends that are also gluten-free. It's kind of simple but it feels non-obvious at the same time.

Suneel: I have to constantly remind myself to be myself. So...how did it all take off from there? What led you from the clubs in New York to the stage at Coachella?

Trevor: At some point I was playing records and there was a booking agent based in New York City who had loved this sound but had moved more into hip-hop. He was like, "This is kind of cool. I don't know anyone else who's doing this kind of thing right now. Do you want to talk some more?" And again, by being myself instead of trying to be what I think he would have liked to hear, that worked out quite nicely.

Suneel: But you're a struggling artist at this point...and now you finally have a shot to play in front of a booking agent. Most people would research the agent, realize he's into hip-hop, and play that. Give him what you know he wants. That seems like the safe approach.

Trevor: Yep. I absolutely agree. It feels pretty obvious. I think one of the major challenges of our time is that we live in this data-driven world. And I think, God bless data, but being data informed, rather than data driven, is probably the best way to be. Where if you can draw a pie chart of all the little chunks of things that you actually are interested in, and then data suggests that one piece of that chart is something that this other person is interested in, great. But I wouldn't so blindly look at data and say, "These people like this thing. I should go be that thing." I think you have to understand who you are and what makes you special.

Suneel: So you found this agent, this backer, Johnny Maroney. What happened from there?

Trevor: Shortly after, I started playing big festivals, from Electric Forest, to giant raves, to New Year's Eve in Beijing, touring Australia. All of those things were a result of someone who was well connected saying, "Hey, I think there's some people that might understand it," and one thing cut into another. Being a part of that early dance music EDM moment meant that, like, Kesha's producers are calling me and we're getting in a room and I'm helping them figure out the live show and touring. Or even working with Katy Perry and going on tour with her and playing arenas for a year straight was a function of me being who I was. Someone who loved pop music, sure, but also was really passionate about house music, and I could kind of connect the dots in an authentic way.

Suneel: Fast-forwarding a few years, how did you bring that level of authenticity to the room when you were pitching investors on your new startup?

Trevor: At the beginning in those original investor presentations, I would say, "Hey, you guys invest in people that don't look like me, don't sound like me. I'm going to try to be the best version of that I can be—instead of being myself." But when I started doing pitches as me and presenting the world that I really wanted to believe in, not what I thought they might want to believe in, that's when things started to work.

Suneel: So in some ways the venture capitalists in the room were like the guys in Yankees hats at the club?

Trevor: Yeah, a little bit. I mean, if you're in a room full of thirteen general partners at a venture fund, you're looking around and you're going, "Okay, Brooks Brothers, Patagonia vest, XY, Allbirds," and you're like, "Okay, I kind of understand culturally what you get excited about. I wonder if I can kind of shoehorn the language of those things into what I do to get you excited." That's absolutely the mistake.

The right way to approach it was I'm going to be who I am and maybe all thirteen of them hate me, but if one of them likes me, perhaps they can get their partners on board or they're going to go, "You know what? I don't think we can do this, but I have a friend that might want to do this," and get you in front of someone who will actually appreciate your business for what it is.

JOHN PALFREY, NONPROFIT LEADER AND EDUCATOR

John is the president of the John D. and Catherine T. Mac-Arthur Foundation, which awards the MacArthur Fellowship, commonly known as the "genius grant." Prior to MacArthur, he served as head of school at Phillips Academy in Andover, Massachusetts, and a dean at Harvard Law School. We spoke to John about being backable from the point of view of admissions. What do he and his team look for in a potential "genius"?

> "I think it's pretty hard to fake real passion. You have a sense that they have really dug deep on something and they are hoping to dig deeper. That it's something where there's real passion behind it as opposed to just kind of the flavor of the month."

Suneel: I've heard MacArthur looks for three qualities when selecting a fellow—originality, insight, and potential. Let's talk about potential. What does that mean to you?

John: It's a really good and interesting question. And in the MacArthur fellows context, it's often asked whether you are just betting on people who are young and therefore have a huge amount ahead of them? And it really doesn't end up translating to age because there are people who hit their strides at very different stages in life and where a certain amount of capital and cachet and support can ensure that they are able to contribute to their fullest. So, I think that potential is comprised of a number of different things, and ultimately, it's a bet.

Suneel: Do you look at potential as something that could happen but isn't currently happening?

John: Sure. It's always about something that hasn't yet happened and that could, that your expectation is that the next thing will be better. And I do think for some people, this places a great deal of pressure on them. The sense that there's an expectation that their next book or their next play or their next concert is going to be that much better. And so there's an implied pressure there, but I do think, yes, that's the idea. There's something that hasn't yet been accomplished and that the world could be improved by virtue of that person having greater opportunity.

Suneel: Does it matter if you think this person would reach their potential with or without you?

John: There's absolutely an analysis that I often think about as a "but for" analysis. So, "but for" this money or "but for" this opportunity, would the person be able to accomplish it? So, let's take, for example, Michelle Obama. She is very likely to do meaningful, creative, innovative things for the rest of her life. She probably has lots of other resources and she's already very famous. So you would be likely to choose somebody who has not yet had the kinds of support or sources of possibility that someone who's already so famous or so capable would have. So, absolutely, there's a sense that we look for opportunities to support someone where, but for our support, they wouldn't be able to accomplish their full potential.

Suneel: Did you use the same "but for" analysis when admitting students to Andover?

John: When you are looking at cases of admission, there are certainly times when you think about who is potentially in the mix of a diverse class, where the things that they could contribute would be so much greater by virtue of being able to have an Andover education and where other students there would have less potential for a variety of reasons; you absolutely consider that.

Suneel: Applicants to a selective program often feel pressure to tout their strengths. But it seems that based on what you are saying, that's not the best strategy.

John: For the MacArthur Fellowship, there's a process of nomination and evaluation and selection, but you can't apply for the fellowship. But let's imagine if you were seeking a grant as opposed to seeking to become a MacArthur fellow, I think that certainly demonstrating a track record is important for everybody. To have a sense of trajectory that somebody who's making a selection decision could observe. But it's not all about everything having been perfect. I think the idea of being able to overcome challenges and to present the fact that you would take full advantage of the resources of a wealthy institution, whether that's a foundation or it's an educational institution, that's a very important piece of the puzzle.

Suneel: Does that mean that you're proactively pointing out your own gap? To describe what you want to accomplish, and express that you can't do it without the program.

John: Absolutely. What would be the value of the education to you and what would you do for the community? It's a combination of those things. You're pointing out the potential; you're pointing out the possibilities and helping the institution see that they could help you accomplish that.

Suneel: Lin-Manuel Miranda, who's a MacArthur fellow, says that "you really have to fall in love with your idea because it's something you're going to be working on for a very long time." How do you suss out if someone is truly in love with their idea?

John: I think it's pretty hard to fake real passion. You have a sense that they have really dug deep on something and they are hoping to dig deeper. That it's something where there's real passion behind it as opposed to just kind of the flavor of the month. And I also think when you look at somebody's CV or résumé, you can get a sense that they stick with stuff for a while. I interviewed somebody today who is not late in her career and she spent fifteen years at the same company doing really interesting things. But I was actually really impressed that she had stuck with something for that period of time and had done it really, really well. So I think that it's a combination of the timbre in the voice and the kind of a sense of resonance of the topic, but also a track record of not just flitting from thing to thing every year. I'm really going deep on something over a period of time. And again, that's the track-record point.

Suneel: If we were to spend a half hour together and you wanted to get a sense of my passion for an idea, what types of questions would you ask?

John: A lot of different questions because I think the topics are going to be really different. So I think it's in part getting somebody to show that they have looked at it in a kaleidoscopic way. They've seen it from lots of different angles and they've really thought about it deeply. And then ultimately if they are really engaged in a topic, if you hit on something that they haven't yet thought about, they often light up. They're like, "Oh my gosh, I haven't thought about that. And I've talked to a thousand people about this and they've never asked that question." I think that's the nature of the half hour that you'd want to spend with them. They are not just being interviewed, but they're actually trying to get something out of you and your questions in their own kind of deep understanding of where the topic is evolving or how it's evolving.

NOTES

INTRODUCTION

1   Alistair Barr and Clare Baldwin, "Groupon's IPO biggest by U.S. Web company since Google," Reuters, November 4, 2011, accessed April 8, 2020, https://www.reuters.com/article/us-groupon/groupons-ipo-biggest-by-u-s-web-company-since-google-idUSTRE7A352020111104.

2   Dominic Rushe, "Groupon fires CEO Andrew Mason after daily coupon company's value tumbles," *Guardian*, February 28, 2013, accessed April 8, 2020, https://www.theguardian.com/technology/2013/feb/28/andrew-mason-leaves-groupon-coupon.

3   Eric Johnson, "Why former Groupon CEO Andrew Mason regrets telling everyone he was fired," *Vox*, December 13, 2017, accessed September 2, 2020, https://www.vox.com/2017/12/13/16770838/groupon-ceo-andrew-mason-descript-audio-startup-recording-word-processor-recode-decode.

4   Howard Berkes, "Challenger engineer who warned of shuttle disaster dies," NPR, February 21, 2016, accessed January 30, 2020, https://www.npr.org/sections/thetwo-way/2016/03/21/470870426/challenger-engineer-who-warned-of-shuttle-disaster-dies. Sarah Kaplan, "Finally free from guilt over Challenger disaster, an engineer dies in peace," *The Washington Post*, March 22, 2016, ac-

cessed August 20, 2020, https://www.washingtonpost.com/news/morning-mix/wp/2016/03/22/finally-free-from-guilt-over-challenger-disaster-an-engineer-dies-in-peace/.

William Grimes, "Robert Ebeling, Challenger Engineer Who Warned of Disaster, Dies at 89," *The New York Times,* March 25, 2020, accessed August 8, 2020, https://www.nytimes.com/2016/03/26/science/robert-ebeling-challenger-engineer-who-warned-of-disaster-dies-at-89.html

5   *Encyclopaedia Britannica Online,* Editors of *Encyclopaedia Britannica,* s.v. "Christa Corrigan McAuliffe," accessed September 2, 2020, https://www.britannica.com/biography/Christa-Corrigan-McAuliffe.

6   Berkes, "Challenger engineer."

7   U.S. Justice Department, U.S. Attorney's Office Southern District of New York, "William McFarland Sentenced To 6 Years In Prison In Manhattan Federal Court For Engaging In Multiple Fraudulent Schemes And Making False Statements To A Federal Law Enforcement Agent," October 11, 2018, accessed September 1, 2020, https://www.justice.gov/usao-sdny/pr/william-mcfarland-sentenced-6-years-prison-manhattan-federal-court-engaging-multiple.

"Fyre: The Greatest Party that Never Happened," Directed by Chris Smith. Originally aired on Netflix, January 18, 2019.

8   *Time,* "Groundbreaker: Damyanti Gupta, First female engineer with an advanced degree at Ford Motor Company," July 29, 2018, accessed August 20, 2020, https://time.com/collection/firsts/5296993/damyanti-gupta-firsts/.

9   *Time,* "Groundbreaker."

10   Dr. Sanjay Gupta, "The Women Who Changed My Life," CNN.com, February 2, 2016, accessed September 2, 2020, https://www.cnn.com/2016/01/13/health/person-who-changed-my-life-sanjay-gupta/index.html.

11   Reshma Saujani, "Girls who code," filmed July 13, 2011, in New York, NY, TED video, 6:49, accessed September 2, 2020, https://youtu.be/ltoLOeE7K4A?t=119.

STEP 1

1   Mark Patinkin, "Mark Patinkin: Recalling when Mister Rogers softened a tough Rhode Island senator," *Providence Journal,* May

31, 2017, accessed September 2, 2020, https://www.providence
journal.com/news/20170531/mark-patinkin-recalling-when
-mister-rogers-softened-tough-rhode-island-senator.

2   "Sir Ken Robinson on how to encourage creativity among students," *CBS This Morning,* March 13, 2019, accessed September 2, 2020, video, 7:02, https://www.youtube.com/watch?v=4DD RNvs6D1I. https://www.ted.com/talks/sir_ken_robinson_do_ schools_kill_creativity.

3   Minda Zetlin, "Elon Musk fails Public Speaking 101. Here's why we hang on every word (and what you can learn from him)," *Inc.,* September 30, 2017, accessed January 28, 2020, https://www .inc.com/minda-zetlin/elon-musk-fails-public-speaking-101-heres -why-we-hang-on-every-word-what-you-can-learn-from-him.html.

4   Mic Wright, "The original iPhone announcement annotated: Steve Jobs' genius meets Genius," Next Web, September 9, 2015, accessed September 2, 2020, https://thenextweb.com/apple /2015/09/09/genius-annotated-with-genius/.

5   "Making life multiplanetary," SpaceX, September 29, 2017, accessed September 2, 2020, video, 1:34, https://www.youtube.com /watch?v=tdUX3ypDVwI.

6   "Mugaritz—back from the brink," *Caterer,* February 17, 2011, accessed September 2, 2020, https://www.thecaterer.com /news/restaurant/mugaritz-back-from-the-brink.

7   The World's 50 Best Restaurants list.

8   Noel Murray, "A new Netflix docuseries heads inside Bill Gates' brain, but it keeps getting sidetracked," *Verge,* September 18, 2019, accessed September 2, 2020, https://www.theverge.com /2019/9/18/20872239/inside-bills-brain-decoding-bill-gates -movie-review-netflix-microsoft-documentary-series.

9   "How to convince investors," August 2013, PaulGraham.com, accessed September 2, 2020, http://paulgraham.com/convince.html.

10   Bel Booker, "Lego's growth strategy: How the toy brand innovated to expand," Attest, September 12, 2019, accessed April 2, 2020, https://www.askattest.com/blog/brand/legos-growth -strategy-how-the-toy-brand-innovated-to-expand.

11   Booker, "Lego's growth strategy."

12   Hillary Dixler Canavan, "Mugaritz is now serving moldy apples," Eater, July 31, 2017, accessed September 2, 2020, https://www

.eater.com/2017/7/31/16069652/mugaritz-noble-rot-moldy
-apples.

13   Elizabeth Foster, "LEGO revenue increases 4% in fiscal 2018,"
Kidscreen, February 27, 2019, accessed April 2, 2020, https
://kidscreen.com/2019/02/27/lego-revenue-increases-4-in
-fiscal-2018/.
Saabira Chaudhuri, "Lego returns to growth as it builds on U.S.
momentum," *Wall Street Journal,* February 27, 2019, accessed
April 2, 2020, https://www.wsj.com/articles/lego-returns-to
-growth-as-it-builds-on-china-expansion-11551259001.

14   "Hello Monday: Troy Carter," LinkedIn Editors, February 26,
2020, video, 33:01, accessed September 2, 2020, https://www
.youtube.com/watch?v=qAtj1HUuZC0.

15   Lisa Robinson, "Lady Gaga's Cultural Revolution," *Vanity Fair,*
September 2010, accessed August 21, 2020, https://archive
.vanityfair.com/article/2010/9/lady-gagas-cultural-revolution.
" 'Pick Yourself Up'—Lady Gaga's West Virginia Roots and Her
Grandma's Inspiring Words That Helped Make a Star," *Moundsville:
Biography of a Classic American Town,* PBS, March 11,
2019, accessed August 21, 2020, https://moundsville.org/2019/
03/11/pick-yourself-up-lady-gagas-west-virginia-roots-and-her
-grandmas-inspiring-words-that-helped-make-a-star/.

16   Joseph Lin, "What diploma? Lady Gaga," Top 10 College Dropouts, *Time,* May 10, 2010, accessed March 23, 2020, http://
content.time.com/time/specials/packages/article/
0,28804,1988080_1988093_1988083,00.html.
Grigoriadis, Vanessa, "Growing Up Gaga," *New York* magazine,
March 26, 2010, accessed August 21, 2020, https://nymag.com
/arts/popmusic/features/65127/.

17   Sissi Cao, "Jeff Bezos and Dwight Schrute both hate PowerPoint,"
Observer, April 19, 2018, accessed September 2, 2020, https://
observer.com/2018/04/why-jeff-bezos-doesnt-allow-powerpoint
-at-amazon-meetings/.

18   Shawn Callahan, "What might Amazon's 6-page narrative structure
look like?" Anecdote, May 8, 2018, accessed September 2, 2020,
https://www.anecdote.com/2018/05/amazons-six-page-narrative
-structure/.

19   Jonathan Haidt, *The Happiness Hypothesis,* Basic Books, Perseus

Book Group, 2006, https://www.happinesshypothesis.com
/happiness-hypothesis-ch1.pdf.

20   "Playwright, composer, and performer Lin-Manuel Miranda, 2015
MacArthur Fellow," MacArthur Foundation, September 28, 2015,
video, 3:25, accessed September 2, 2020, https://youtu.be
/r69-fohpJ3o?t=15.

21   Vinamrata Singal, "Introducing Jimmy Chen—Propel," Medium, August 8, 2017, accessed September 2, 2020, https://
medium.com/social-good-of-silicon-valley/introducing-jimmy
-chen-propel-ed02c3014e75.

STEP 2

1   Eric Savitz, "Kirsten Green," *Barron's,* March 20, 2020, accessed September 2, 2020, https://www.barrons.com/articles/barrons-100
-most-influential-women-in-u-s-finance-kirsten-green-51584709202.
Kirsten Green, "Empowerment: Forerunner and Fund IV," Medium, October 8, 2018, accessed September 2, 2020, https://
medium.com/forerunner-insights/empowerment-forerunner-at
-fund-iv-1dd0cc1b6bc9.

2   Dave Nussbaum, "Writing to persuade: Insights from former New
York Times op-ed editor Trish Hall," *Behavioral Scientist,* March 16,
2020, accessed September 2, 2020, https://behavioralscientist
.org/writing-to-persuade-insights-from-former-new-york-times-op
-ed-editor-trish-hall/.

3   *Inside Bill's Brain,* episode 2, directed by Davis Guggenheim, released September 20, 2019, on Netflix.

4   Stephanie Rosenbloom, "The World According to Tim Ferriss,"
New York Times, March 25, 2011, accessed August 19, 2020,
https://www.nytimes.com/2011/03/27/fashion/27Ferris.html?
src=twrhp.

5   Tim Ferriss, The Tim Ferriss Show Transcripts: The 4-Hour
Workweek Revisited (#295), February 6, 2018, accessed September 2, 2020, https://tim.blog/2018/02/06/the-tim-ferriss
-show-transcripts-the-4-hour-workweek-revisited/.

6   "Here's how Airbnb and Pixar use storytelling to bring
great experiences to travelers," Next Generation Customer
Experience, accessed September 2, 2020, https://nextgencx

.wbresearch . com / airbnb - pixar - use-storytelling-better-travel -experience-ty-u.

7   Sarah Kessler, "How Snow White helped Airbnb's mobile mission," *Fast Company,* November 8, 2012, accessed September 2, 2020, https://www.fastcompany.com/3002813/how-snow-white -helped-airbnbs-mobile-mission.

8   DocSend and Tom Eisenmann, "What We Learned From 200 Startups Who Raised $360M," July 2015, accessed August 21, 2020, https://docsend.com/view/p8jxsqr.

9   Russ Heddleston, "Data tells us that investors love a good story," *TechCrunch,* April 12, 2019, accessed September 2, 2020, https:// techcrunch.com/2019/04/12/data - tells - us-that-investors-love-a -good-story/.

10 Christopher Steiner, "Groupon's Andrew Mason did what great founders do," *Forbes,* February 28, 2013, accessed September 2, 2020, https : // www . forbes . com / sites / christophersteiner / 2013 /02 /28/groupons - andrew - mason - did - what - great-founders - do /#89ff8d58810d.

11 Eric Newcomer, "In video, Uber CEO argues with driver over falling fares," *Bloomberg,* February 28, 2017, accessed September 2, 2020, https://www.bloomberg.com/news /articles/2017-02-28/in-video - uber - ceo - argues-with-driver -over-falling-fares.

12 Johana Bhuiyan, "A new video shows Uber CEO Travis Kalanick arguing with a driver over fares," *Vox,* February 28, 2017, accessed May 1, 2020, https://www.vox.com/2017/2/28/14766964 /video-uber-travis-kalanick-driver-argument.

STEP 3

1   September 2, 2020, https://a16z.com/2018/08/04/earned -secrets-ben-horowitz-interns-2018/ (start at 8:15).

2   https://getpaidforyourpad.com/blog/the - airbnb -founder-story /#:~:text=It's%20late%202007%20in%20San,just%20moved%20 from%20New%20York.&text=They%20bought%20a%20few%20 airbeds,and%20breakfast%20in%20the%20morning.

3   Steven Levitt, "The freakonomics of crack dealing," filmed February 2004 in Monterey, California, TED video, 21:03, accessed

September 2, 2020, https://www.ted.com/talks/steven_levitt _the_freakonomics_of_crack_dealing/transcript?language=en.

4 Jessica Bennett, "Inside a Notorious Street Gang," *Newsweek,* January 31, 2008, accessed August 23, 2020, https://www.newsweek .com/inside-notorious-street-gang-86603.

"Researcher Studies Gangs by Leading One," NPR, January 12, 2008, retrieved August 23, 2020, https://www.npr.org /transcripts/18003654.

5 Shannon Bond, "Logan Green, the carpooling chief executive driving Lyft's IPO," *Financial Times,* March 8, 2019, accessed August 24, 2020, https://www.ft.com/content/8a55de94-414e -11e9-b896-fe36ec32aece.

Mike Isaac and Kate Conger, "As I.P.O Approaches, Lyft CEO Is Nudged into the Spotlight," *New York Times,* January 27, 2019, accessed September 1, 2020, https://www.nytimes.com/2019 /01/27/technology/lyft-ceo-logan-green.html.

6 Nick Romano, "Howard Stern to release first book in more than 20 years," *Entertainment Weekly,* March 12, 2019, accessed January 29, 2020, https://ew.com/books/2019/03/12/howard -stern-comes-again-book/.

7 "Simon & Schuster's Jonathan Karp Calls Howard Stern His White Whale," The Howard Stern Show, May 14, 2019, retrieved January 28, 2020, https://www.youtube.com/watch?v =BOddXs4uzxc.

STEP 4

1 Malcolm Lewis, "AirBnB pitch deck," March 12, 2015, slide 4, accessed September 2, 2020, https://www.slideshare.net /PitchDeckCoach/airbnb-first-pitch-deck-editable.

2 "Rent the Runway: Jenn Hyman," *How I Built This with Guy Raz,* NPR, August 7, 2017, retrieved August 18, 2020, https:// www.npr.org/2017/09/21/541686055/rent-the-runway-jenn -hyman.

3 Adrian Granzella Larssen, "What we've learned: A Q&A with Rent the Runway's founders," *The Muse,* accessed September 2, 2020, https://www.themuse.com/advice/what-weve-learned-a -qa-with-rent-the-runways-founders.

4   Kantar, Worldpanel Division US, Beverages Consumption Panel, 12 March 2014.

5   Daniel Kahneman, "Daniel Kahneman," Biographical, The Nobel Prize, 2002, accessed August 25, 2020, https://www.nobelprize .org/prizes/economic-sciences/2002/kahneman/biographical/. Amos Tversky and Daniel Kahneman, "Loss Aversion in Risk-less Choice: A Reference-Dependent Model," *The Quarterly Journal of Economics* 106, 4 (November 1991): 1039–1061, https://doi.org/10.2307/2937956.

6   Minda Zetlin, "Blockbuster could have bought Netflix for $50 million, but the CEO thought it was a joke," *Inc.*, September 20, 2019, accessed September 2, 2020, https://www.inc.com /minda-zetlin/netflix-blockbuster-meeting-marc-randolph-reed -hastings-john-antioco.html Marc Randolph, "He 'was struggling not to laugh': Inside Netflix's crazy, doomed meeting with Blockbuster," *Vanity Fair*, September 17, 2019, accessed September 2, 2020, https://www.vanityfair.com/ news/2019/09/netflixs-crazy-doomed-meeting-with-blockbuster.

7   Bill Cotter, *Seattle's 1962 World's Fair* (Mount Pleasant, SC: Arcadia, 2015), 28, accessed September 2, 2020, https://books .google.com/books?id=LefRCgAAQBAJ&pg = PA27&lpg = PA27 &dq=In + 1962,+General+Motors+showcased + its + Firebird+III& source = bl&ots = kcVBkz9SCX&sig = ACfU3U2ZV_NV-fQQcqg INenD8l3jsWH6fw&hl = en&sa = X&ved=2ahUKEwj0tdT0pdDp AhUBgnIEHc2hBBEQ6AEwC3oECAsQAQ#v = onepage&q=In %201962%2C%20General%20Motors%20showcased%20its%20Fir ebird%20III&f=false.

8   Matt Novak, "GM Car of the Future," Paleofuture, https://paleofu ture.com/blog/2007/6/29/gm-car-of-the-future-1962.html.

9   Dan Primack and Kirsten Korosec, "GM buying self-driving tech startup for more than $1 billion," *Fortune*, March 11, 2016, ac-cessed September 2, 2020, https://fortune.com/2016/03/11 /gm-buying-self-driving-tech-startup-for-more-than-1-billion/.

10   "Ford invests in Argo AI, a new artificial intelligence company, in drive for autonomous vehicle leadership," Ford Media Center, February 10, 2017, accessed September 2, 2020, https://media .ford.com/content/fordmedia/fna/us/en/news/2017/02/10 /ford-invests-in-argo-ai-new-artificial-intelligence-company.html.

11   Megan Rose Dickey, "Waymo expands autonomous driving partnership with Fiat Chrysler," *TechCrunch,* May 31, 2018, accessed September 2, 2020, https://techcrunch.com/2018/05/31/waymo-expands-autonomous-driving-partnership-with-fiat-chrysler/.

12   "Uber to use self-driving Mercedes-Benz cars," Fleet Europe, February 1, 2017, accessed September 2, 2020, https://www.fleeteurope.com/fr/connected-financial-models-smart-mobility/europe/news/uber-use-self-driving-mercedes-benz-cars?a=FJA05&t%5B0%5D=Daimler&t%5B1%5D=Mercedes-Benz&t%5B2%5D=Uber&curl=1.

13   Jefferies, "The Millennial's New Clothes: Apparel Rental and the Impact to Retailers," August 19, 2019, https://drive.google.com/file/d/1dzBxn1l213S9Ew4BqeWOn_Ky-4sGaNdz/view.

14   Case study: https://www.zuora.com/our-customers/case-studies/zoom/.

15   Sarah Lacy, "Amazon buys Zappos; the price is $928m., not $847m.," *TechCrunch,* July 22, 2009, accessed September 2, 2020, https://techcrunch.com/2009/07/22/amazon-buys-zappos/.

16   Collen DeBaise, "Cinderella dreams, shoestring budget? No problem," *Wall Street Journal,* February 16, 2011, accessed January 28, 2020, https://www.wsj.com/articles/SB10001424052748703373404576148170681457268.

17   Jessica Klein, "35% of the U.S. workforce is now freelancing—10 million more than 5 years ago," *Fast Company,* October 3, 2019, accessed September 2, 2020, https://www.fastcompany.com/90411808/35-of-the-u-s-workforce-is-now-freelancing-10-million-more-than-5-years-ago.

18   Dakin Campbell, "How WeWork spiraled from a $47 billion valuation to talk of bankruptcy in just 6 weeks," *Business Insider,* September 28, 2019, accessed September 2, 2020, https://www.businessinsider.com/weworks-nightmare-ipo.

19   Madeline Cuello, "What is the gig economy?" WeWork, November 27, 2019, accessed January 30, 2019, https://www.wework.com/ideas/what-is-the-gig-economy.

20   Eliot Brown, "How Adam Neumann's Over-the-Top Style Built WeWork: 'This Is Not the Way Everybody Behaves,' " *The Wall Street Journal,* September 18, 2019, retrieved August 20, 2020,

https://www.wsj.com/articles/this-is-not-the-way-everybody
-behaves-how-adam-neumanns-over-the-top-style-built-wework
-11568823827.

21 Gary Krakow, "Happy birthday, Palm Pilot," MSNBC.com,
March 22, 2006, accessed January 30, 2020, http://www
.nbcnews.com/id/11945300/ns/technology_and_science-tech
_and_gadgets/t/happy-birthday-palm-pilot/.

22 Alexis Madrigal, "The iPhone was inevitable," *Atlantic,* June 29, 2017,
accessed January 30, 2020, https://www.theatlantic.com/technology
/archive/2017/06/the-iphone-was-inevitable/531963/.

STEP 5

1 Laura Spinney, "The hard way: Our odd desire to do it ourselves," *New Scientist,* December 20, 2011, accessed September
2, 2020, https://www.newscientist.com/article/mg21228441
-800-the-hard-way-our-odd-desire-to-do-it-ourselves/.

2 Michael I. Norton, Daniel Mochon, and Dan Ariely, "The 'IKEA
effect': When labor leads to love" (working paper 11-091, Harvard Business School, 2011), accessed September 2, 2020,
https://www.hbs.edu/faculty/publication%20files/11-091.pdf.

3 Norton, Mochon, and Ariely, "The 'IKEA effect.'"

4 Salman Rushdie, *Midnight's Children* (London: Everyman's
Library, 1995).

5 Phil Alexander, "One Louder!", *Mojo,* February 2010, p. 77.

6 Matthew Creamer, "Apple's first marketing guru on why '1984' is
overrated," *AdAge,* March 1, 2012, accessed January 28, 2020,
https://adage.com/article/digital/apple-s-marketing-guru-1984
-overrated/232933.

7 "Steve Jobs: The man in the machine," CNN, January 9,
2016, accessed January 28, 2020, https://archive.org
/details/CNNW_20160110_020000_Steve_Jobs_The_Man
_in_the_Machine/start/1080/end/1140.

8 Regis McKenna, "My biggest mistake: Regis McKenna," *Indepen-
dent,* November 11, 1992, accessed January 28, 2020, https://
www.independent.co.uk/news/business/my-biggest-mistake-regis
-mckenna-1556795.html.

9 Sarah Buhr, "Piper Pied imitates HBO's Silicon Valley and creates

lossless compression for online images," *TechCrunch,* May 3, 2015, accessed September 2, 2020, https://techcrunch.com/2015/05 /03/ppiper-pied-imitates-hbos-silicon-valley-and-creates-lossless -compression-for-online-images/.

Kyle Russell, "Facebook acquires QuickFire Networks, a 'Pied Piper' for video," *TechCrunch,* January 8, 2015, accessed September 2, 2020, https://techcrunch.com/2015/01/08/facebook -acquires-quickfire-networks-a-pied-piper-for-video/.

10 "Inaugural address of John F. Kennedy," January 20, 1961, Avalon Project, Yale Law School, accessed September 2, 2020, https:// avalon.law.yale.edu/20th_century/kennedy.asp.

11 "MBA entering class profile," Stanford Graduate School of Business, accessed September 2, 2020, https://www.gsb.stanford.edu /programs/mba/admission/class-profile.

12 https://www.aspeninstitute.org/programs/henry-crown-fellowship /nominate-henry-crown-fellowship/

13 Amy Larocca, "The magic skin of Glossier's Emily Weiss," *New York* magazine, January 8, 2018, accessed September 2, 2020, https://www.thecut.com/2018/01/glossier-emily-weiss .html.

14 Staff of Entrepreneur Media, *Entrepreneur Voices on Growth Hacking* (Irvine, CA: Entrepreneur Press, 2018), accessed September 2, 2020, https://books.google.com/books?id=6KBT DwAAQBAJ&pg=PT126&lpg=PT126&dq=into+the+gloss+ten +million+page+views&source=bl&ots=yilRPWW8Sn&sig=ACf U3U0Y0CPWr8M6JS87mnmRtejfARRx7w&hl=en&sa=X&ved =2ahUKEwjiqMnOm9DpAhVrkeAKHbP_D6kQ6AEwCXoECA oQAQ#v=onepage&q=into%20the%20gloss%20ten%20million% 20page%20views&f=false.

15 Staff of Entrepreneur Media, *Entrepreneur Voices on Growth Hacking.*

16 Anthony Noto, "Kirsten Green's Forerunner Ventures raises $350M," *Business Journals,* October 9, 2018, accessed September 2, 2020, https://www.bizjournals.com/bizwomen/news/latest -news/2018/10/kirsten-greens-forerunner-ventures-raises-350m .html.

17 Bridget March, "Glossier is now valued at more than $1.2 billion," *Harper's Bazaar,* March 20, 2019, accessed September 2,

2020, https://www.harpersbazaar.com/uk/beauty/make-up -nails/a26881951/glossier-valuation-unicorn/.

Lawrence Ingrassia, "Meet the Investor Who Bet Early on Warby Parker, Glossier, and Dollar Shave Club," Medium, February 13, 2020, accessed August 26, 2020, https://marker.medium.com/meet -the-investor-who-bet-early-on-warby-parker-dollar-shave-club-and -glossier-9809fc9ea1e.

18   Polina Marinova, "Stitch Fix CEO Katrina Lake joins the board of beauty products company Glossier," *Fortune,* June 26, 2018, accessed September 2, 2020, https://fortune.com/2018/06/26 /katrina-lake-stitchfix-glossier/.

19   Masters of Scale, "The Reid Hoffman Story (Part 2) Make Everyone a Hero," https://mastersofscale.com/wp-content/uploads /2019/02/mos-episode-transcript-reid-hoffman-part-2.pdf.

20   Penelope Burk, *Donor-Centered Fundraising, Second Edition* (Chicago: Cygnus Applied Research Inc., 2018), https://cygresearch .com/product/donor-centered-fundraising-new-edition/.

STEP 6

1   Hunter Walk, "Do it in real time: Practicing your startup pitch," *Hunter Walk* (blog), July 25, 2019, accessed September 2, 2020, https://hunterwalk.com/2019/07/25/do-it-in-real -time-practicing-your-startup-pitch/.

2   Life Healthcare, Inc. (form S-1 registration statement, U.S. Securities and Exchange Commission, January 3, 2020), accessed September 2, 2020, https://www.sec.gov/Archives/edgar/data /1404123/000119312520001429/d806726ds1.htm.

3   Melia Robinson, "After trying One Medical, I could never use a regular doctor again," *Business Insider,* January 28, 2016, accessed January 29, 2020, https://www.businessinsider.com/ what-its-like-to-use-one-medical-group-2016-1#the-freedom -to-easily-see-a-doctor-in-40-locations-nationwide-makes-one -medical-group-the-best-practice-ive-ever-used-22.

4   "The World's 50 Most Innovative Companies 2017," *Fast Company,* accessed September 2, 2020, https://www.fastcompany .com/most-innovative-companies/2017/sectors/health.

5   Esther Perel, "The secret to desire in a long-term relationship,"

TEDSalon NY 2013, https://www.ted.com/talks/esther_perel _the_secret_to_desire_in_a_long_term_relationship/transcript? language=en#t-247887.

6   "The Tim Ferriss Show transcripts: Episode 28: Peter Thiel (show notes and links at tim.blog/podcast)," 2017–2018, accessed September 2, 2020, https://tim.blog/wp-content/uploads/2018 /07/28-peter-thiel.pdf.

7   "Charlie Munger on Getting Rich, Wisdom, Focus, Fake Knowledge and More," https://fs.blog/2017/02/charlie-munger-wisdom/.

8   "Obama 4: Wait Your Turn," from *Making Obama*, Chicago Public Media, March 1, 2018, accessed September 2, 2020, https:// www.wbez.org/stories/obama-4-wait-your-turn/34d62aec-cd06 -49bc-86a6-4cdf33766055

9   John Sepulvado, "Obama's 'overnight success' in 2004 was a year in the making," OPB, May 19, 2016, accessed September 2, 2020, https://www.opb.org/news/series/election-2016 /president-barack-obama-2004-convention-speech-legacy/.

10   Jodi Kantor and Monica Davey, "Crossed Paths: Chicago's Jacksons and Obamas," *New York Times*, February 24, 2013, accessed September 1, 2020, https://www.nytimes.com/2013/02/25 /us/politics/crossed-paths-chicagos-jacksons-and-obamas.html.

11   "Obama 1: The Man in the Background," from *Making Obama*, Chicago Public Media, February 8, 2018, accessed September 2, 2020, https://www.wbez.org/stories/obama-1-the-man-in-the -background/52566713-83d4-4875-8bb1-eba55937228e.

STEP 7

1   "George P. Schaller, PhD: Wildlife Biologist and Conservationist," Biography, Academy of Achievement, accessed August 20, 2020, https://achievement.org/achiever/george-b-schaller -ph-d/.
"Jack Kornfield: Awakening the Buddha of Wisdom in Difficulties," accessed August 28, 2020, https://jackkornfield.com /awakening-buddha-wisdom-difficulties/.
Jack Kornfield, *A Lamp in the Darkness: Illuminating the Path Through Difficult Times* (Sounds True, 2014).

2   "Pizza trivia," Pizza Joint website, accessed September 2, 2020,

https://www.thepizzajoint.com/pizzafacts.html, and Packaged Facts, New York.

3 Yoni Blumberg, "Domino's stock outperformed Apple and Amazon over 7 years—now it's the world's largest pizza chain," CNBC, March 1, 2018, accessed January 30, 2020, https://www.cnbc.com/2018/03/01/no-point-1-pizza-chain-dominos-outperformed-amazon-google-and-apple-stocks.html.

4 Parmy Olson, "Inside The Facebook–WhatsApp Megadeal: The Courtship, The Secret Meetings, The $19 Billion Poker Game," *Forbes,* March 4, 2014, accessed August 20, 2020, https://www.forbes.com/sites/parmyolson/2014/03/04/inside-the-facebook-whatsapp-megadeal-the-courtship-the-secret-meetings-the-19-billion-poker-game/#2a3c0945350f.

5 Peter Kelley, "The King's Speech mostly true to life, UW expert on stuttering says," *UW News,* January 12, 2001, accessed January 28, 2020, https://www.washington.edu/news/2011/01/12/the-kings-speech-mostly-true-to-life-uw-expert-on-stuttering-says/.

6 "Charges baby food maker utilized scare tactics," *Standard-Speaker* (Hazleton, Pennsylvania), January 10, 1976, p. 8, accessed September 24, 2020, https://www.newspapers.com/clip/23773011/.

7 Adam Braun, *The Promise of a Pencil* (New York: Scribner, 2014), 122–123.

CONCLUSION

1 "Airbnb statistics," iProperty Management, last updated March 2020, accessed September 1, 2020, https://ipropertymanagement.com/research/airbnb-statistics.

APPENDIX 2

1 Interviews have been excerpted and edited for clarity.

INDEX

A

Adichie, Chimamanda Ngozi, 82–83
Aduriz, Andoni, 18–19, 21, 23, 137
advisers, 104–108
advocates, 76–77, 121–126
"agent" mindset, 118
Airbnb, 40–41, 50, 58, 142
  inevitability of, 63
  theme of, 197–198
Amazon, 25–26
Andreessen Horowitz, 50
anthropology, armchair, 62–66, 142, 178–179, 181
Apollo 13 (film), 192–194, 195, 196, 197
Apple, 24
  autonomous vehicle, 68
  brand identity for, 80
  iPhone, 16, 65, 72–73, 143
  Rise pitch to, 124–126
Aspen Institute Henry Crown Fellowship Program, 83
audience, 35–38
authenticity, 207–212
autonomous vehicles, 67–68
Away, 39, 42

B

BabyCenter, 62, 63, 174
backability, 9
  casting a central character and, 33–47
  convincing yourself first, 15–32
  developing, 10, 14
  earned secrets and, 48–60
  exhibition matches and, 94–113
  flipping outsiders to insiders and, 75–93
  letting go of ego and, 114–126
  mistakes in, 153–154
  sense of inevitability and, 61–74
  summary of steps toward, 137–145
backable circles, 104–108, 146
backers
  as advocates, 76–77
  emotional connection to ideas and, 31–32
  empathy bridges with, 41–42
  flipping outsiders to insiders and, 75–93
  loss aversion and, 66–70
  making them into heroes, 85–90
  showing your effort to, 54–60

Baskin, Roberta, 120
A Beautiful Mind (film), 194
Beech-Nut, 120
Benchmark Capital, 186
Berg, Alec, 81
Berners-Lee, Tim, 82–83
Bezos, Jeff, 25–26
Black Kings gang, 52
Bodow, Steve, 103
Bonobos, 70–71, 141, 183–190
Booker, Cory, 83
brain systems, 30–32, 34–35, 126
branding, 168–169
Brandless, 176
Braun, Adam, 123–124
breakfast cereal, 176, 178, 182
Brin, Sergey, 101
Brud, 207
Buck's of Woodside, 127–129
bullet points, 26
Burk, Penelope, 86–87
"but for" test, 83, 214–215

C
cake mixes, instant, 75–76
Cameron, James, 50–51,
    139–140, 155, 160–161
Canada, Chelsea, 123–124
Carter, Troy, 23
case building, 192–194
Catmull, Ed, 95
CBS, 78–79, 91
central characters, 33–47, 139
    based on your reader/audience,
        35–38
    keeping in sight, 43–47
    for Rise, 45–47
    storyboards and, 39–43
Challenger space shuttle, 11,
    185–186
charisma, 16
Cheddars, 107–108, 144
cheerleaders, 107
Chernin, Peter, 17, 51, 157–167
Chernin Group, 155

Chesky, Brian, 40, 50, 58,
    195–196
coaches, 106–107
Cohen, June, 86
collaboration, in pitches, 80–82
collaborators, 105–106
Colonna, Jerry, 125
Comcast, 68–69, 141
Comedy Cellar, 97–98
commitment, 201–202
Conduit, 88–89
confidence
    letting go of ego and, 118–119
    practice and, 109–111
conviction, 16–17, 164,
    174–177. *See also* convincing
    yourself first
convincing yourself first, 15–32,
    137, 138, 204–205
    emotional connection and,
        30–32
    incubation time and, 18–23
    steering into objections and,
        24–27
    throwing away work and,
        28–30
Cook, Tim, 124
cookware, chemical-free,
    189–190
Couchsurfing.com, 140
Craigslist, 140
creativity, 75, 164–165
    the "but for" test and, 83
credibility, 160–162
critics, 107–108
Cruise Automation, 68
Cuban, Mark, 106
culture
    central characters and, 45
    seeing trends in, 61–66
customer experience, 39–43,
    150–151
customers, connections with,
    190

D

The Daily Show (TV show), 103
Dallas Mavericks, 106
Dark Waters (film), 189–190
deadlines, for incubation time, 23
decision making, loss aversion in, 66–70
Democratic National Convention, 109–110
Dichter, Ernest, 75–76
Dingell, John, 87–88
discipline, 23
Disney, 40
DJ Skeet Skeet. *See* McFedries, Trevor
DocSend, 42–43
Dollar Shave Club, 33–34, 35, 39–40, 42, 139, 149–154
Domino's Pizza, 115–116
Dorsey, Jack, 9, 95–96
Dotan, Jonathan, 80–83
Dubin, Michael, 33–34, 35, 39–40, 42, 139, 149–154
Dubner, Stephen J., 52, 58
Dunn, Andy, 70–71, 141, 183–191
DuPont, 189–190

E

earned secrets, 48–60, 139–140
    definition of, 50
    going beyond Google for, 51–54
    how you arrive at an idea and, 50–51
    showing your effort and, 54–60
Ebeling, Bob, 11
effort, showing your, 54–60, 140
ego, letting go of, 114–126, 145
    finding the passionate few and, 121–126, 209–211
    forgetting yourself and, 117–120
    showing vs. telling and, 115–117

8 Mile (film), 107, 194
embarrassment, 100–101, 145
emotional connection, 138
    backable circles and, 104–108
    with central characters, 34–35
    with customers, 40–43
    feeling like a hero and, 86–88
    with ideas, 30–32
"Emotional Rotten Tomatoes," 106–107
empathy bridges, 41, 139
enthusiasm, 157–159
Eschmeyer, Evan, 105–106
execution, 75
exhibition matches, 94–113, 143–144
experimentation, 21, 27
extroverts, 157–159, 203–204

F

Facebook, 116–117
facts and figures, 42–43, 194–195
Fadell, Tony, 73
failure, 133, 134
Failure Conference (FailCon), 5–6, 7–9, 134
fear, 125–126
fear of missing out (FOMO), 67–70, 141
feedback
    changing style based on, 111–113
    getting in-depth, 101–104, 143–144
    negative, 100–101
    nonverbal, 103–104, 180
    showing the impact of, 88–90
    steering into objections and, 24–27
    your backable circle and, 104–108
Ferriss, Tim, 36, 139
financial runway, 30
Finding Nemo (film), 99
Firefox, 6–7

Fitzgerald, Ella, 109
flexitarian diets, 65–66
Floodgate, 200
FOMO. *See* fear of missing out (FOMO)
Ford Motor Company, 12–13, 68, 131–132
Forerunner Ventures, 33–34, 148–154
The 4-Hour Workweek (Ferriss), 36, 141
Freakonomics (Dubner & Levitt), 52, 58
Friday Night Lights (TV show), 194
Fyre Festival, 11–12

G
Gaga, Lady, 23
Game of Now, 127–133
gangs, economics of, 51–52
Gates, Bill, 19, 35–36, 41
Gebbia, Joe, 50
generalization, 196–197
General Magic, 73
General Motors, 67–68
genius, untapped, 11, 130
"genius grants," 82–83
getting started, 28–29, 127–133
Girls Who Code, 13
Google, 68, 90–91, 100–101
Gore, Al, 112
Graham, Paul, 19
Grant, Rylend, 92–93
Grazer, Brian, 52–53, 129, 140, 192–199
Green, Kirsten, 33–34, 35, 85, 139, 148–154
Green, Logan, 53–54, 202–203, 205–206
Greenblatt, Bob, 162, 163–164
Green Triangle case, 185–186
Gretzky, Wayne, 73, 141
Groupon, 7, 32, 43–44, 104, 139
Guggenheim, David, 31–32, 77–78

Gupta, Leena, 106–107
Gupta, Sanjay, 7–8, 132–133
Gupta, Subhash, 132

H
Haas, Derek, 92–93
Haidt, Jonathan, 30–31
Hall, Trish, 35
The Happiness Hypothesis (Haidt), 30–31
Harper, Tommy, 78
Harvard Business School, 42–43, 76, 165
Hastings, Reed, 83
Heddleston, Russ, 42–43
heroes, 85–90, 142
Hingorani, Damyanti, 12–13
Hoffman, Reid, 24–25, 100, 138
Horowitz, Ben, 50, 58
Howard, Ron, 129
Howard Stern Comes Again (Karp), 57–58
human traits, 185–186
Hyman, Jennifer, 63–64, 69

I
IBM, 73
ideas
    casting a central character for, 33–47
    creating ownership of, 75–78
    emotional connection with, 30–32
    how you arrive at, 50–51
    incubation time for, 18–23
    researching, 48–60
    sharing just enough and, 90–93
    sharing prematurely, 21
    showing inevitability of, 69–70
    throwing away uncompelling, 28–30
identity, 207–212
"IKEA effect," 76
Imagine Entertainment, 52–53, 129, 192

impact, helping people
  understand their, 86–88
An Inconvenient Truth (film), 31,
  77–78
incubation time, 18–23, 27, 137
inevitability, 61–74, 140–141
  armchair anthropology and,
    62–66
  loss aversion and, 66–70
  Method and, 167–169
  Sharkey on, 176–178
  showing momentum and, 70–71
  vision and, 71–74
Inside Bill's Brain (TV show), 31
insiders, creating, 75–93
insight, 51–54
Instagram, 121
interviews, 147
  with Chernin, 155–165
  with Dunn, 183–190
  with Grazer, 192–199
  with Green, 148–154
  with Lowry, 166–173
  with McFedries, 207–212
  with Palfrey, 213–217
  with Sharkey, 174–182
Into the Gloss blog, 84–85
introverts, 157–159, 203–204
Isaacs, James, 24
It Might Get Loud (film), 77–78
iVillage, 62–63, 174

J
Jackson, Jesse, 113
Jacob, Oren, 94–96, 99
Jacobs, A. J., 126
JibJab, 119
Jobs, Steve, 16, 72–73, 80, 94,
  95, 141
Jones, James Earl, 118
Judge, Mike, 81

K
Kahani Movement, 24
Kahneman, Daniel, 66

Kalanick, Travis, 45
Kapoor, Raj, 205
Karp, Jonathan, 56–58, 142
Kennedy, John F., 82
kindness, 208
Knapp, Jake, 90–91, 142–143
Kombis, 53–54

L
Lachapelle, Serge, 90–91
Lands' End, 188
Lee, Tom, 102–103, 145
LEGO, 21–22, 23
Levitt, Steven, 51–52, 58
Lil Miquela, 121
Lin, Justin, 93
LinkedIn, 24, 25, 138
Linkner, Josh, 109–110, 200,
  202–203, 205–206
listening, 179–180
Lobo (film), 91–92
loss aversion, 66–70
Lovell, Jim, 193
Lowry, Adam, 61–62, 63, 65–66,
  69, 166–173
Lyft, 45, 53–54, 200–201,
  202–203, 205–206

M
MacArthur Foundation "genius
  grants," 82–83, 144,
  213–217
"Mack the Knife" (song), 109
MacNiven, Jamis, 127–129
Madoff, Bernie, 91–93
Manning, Sean, 57
Marcelli, Rémi, 21–22, 23
Maroney, Johnny, 211
marriage, expectations about,
  104–105
Mars (TV show), 196–197
Mason, Andrew, 7, 43–44
McAuliffe, Christa, 11
McClelland, Ted, 113
McFarland, Billy, 11–12

McFedries, Trevor, 121–123, 207–212
McKenna, Regis, 80
Method, 61–62, 63, 65–66, 69, 71, 166–173
Michigan, 133
Miranda, Lin-Manuel, 31, 82–83
Miura-Ko, Ann, 54, 200–206
momentum, 70–71, 141
Monroe, Marilyn, 118
mountain gorillas, 114
Mozilla, 6–7
Mugaritz restaurant, 18–19, 21, 137
Murdoch, Rupert, 159
Musk, Elon, 16, 196

N
narrative. *See* storytelling
National Geospatial-Intelligence Agency, 88–89
Net Promoter Score, 102–103
Neumann, Adam, 72–73
New York Times, 8–9, 134
Nixon, Richard M., 15–16
Nokia, 73
nonverbal feedback, 103–104, 180
Nortman, Kara, 122–123
Norton, Michael, 76

O
Obama, Barack, 10, 111–113, 144
objections, steering into, 24–27, 137–139, 159–160, 179–180
One Medical, 10, 102–103, 130–131
openness, 160
originality, 196–197, 213–214
Ornekian, Dikran, 91–93
outsiders, flipping to insiders, 75–93, 141–143

making them into heroes and, 85–90
sharing just enough and, 90–93
by sharing what it could be, 78–82
the story of us in, 82–85
ownership, 76–78

P
Page, Jimmy, 77–78, 142
Page, Larry, 101
Palfrey, John, 82–83, 213–217
Parker, Charlie, 117
passion
finding supporters with, 121–126, 145, 209–211
having your own before creating it in others, 30
questions to elicit, 219
testing, 163
throwing away uninspiring ideas and, 28–30
Pastore, John, 15
PBS. *See* Public Broadcasting Service (PBS)
Pencils of Promise, 123–124
Pentagon, 88–89, 142
Perel, Esther, 104
persistence, 30, 124, 205–206
personality, 100–101, 157–159, 160–162, 203, 205–206
Peterson, Joel, 183–191
Pink, Dan, 101
pitches
active listening in, 179–180
at Amazon, 25–26
as back-and-forth vs. monologue, 17, 80–82
backup section in, 80
customizing vs. shoe-horning, 123
facts/figures vs. storytelling in, 42–43
incubation time before, 22–23
insight in and behavior shifts after, 178–179

knowing your audience for, 35–38

letting go of ego for, 114–126

practicing, 94–113

showing momentum in, 70–71

showing your effort in, 54–60

slides in, 25–26

storyboards for, 39–43

storytelling in, 26

Pixar, 94–96, 99

pizza-delivery app, 115–116

Pollan, Michael, 65–66

Popcorn Fiction, 92–93

potential, 83, 213–217

practice, 94–113, 143–144, 179

getting real feedback on, 101–104

negative feedback and, 100–101

rule of 21 on, 109–111

in small venues, 97–99

your backable circle and, 104–108

products, adding, 186–187

Public Broadcasting Service (PBS), 15–16

Pumpkin Pie, 189–190

R

Rachleff, Andy, 186

Rainbow PUSH, 113

Rashid, Karim, 62

rationality, 30–32

readiness, 131–132

Reboot: Leadership and the Art of Growing Up (Colonna), 125

recovery muscle, 109, 144

rejection, 10, 36, 55, 57, 67, 119–120, 124

relationships, expectations about, 104–105

Rent the Runway, 63–64, 69, 71, 177–179, 181

research, 48–60, 139–142, 161

in flipping outsiders to insiders, 84

going beyond Google with, 51–54

Ripple, 66, 164, 172–173

Rise, 130–131

acquired by One Medical, 10, 102

Apple pitch for, 124–126

backup section of pitch for, 80

central character for, 45–47

customer acquisition for, 26–27

FailCon and, 5–6

feedback on, 89–90

incubation time for, 22–23

inevitability and, 73–74

key partnerships for, 117–118

pitch practice for, 108

prototypical customer for, 41–42

showing effort in the pitch for, 58–60

showing the inevitability of, 65

steering into objections to, 26–27

Roberts, Jordan, 116–117

Robinson, Sir Ken, 16

Rogers, Fred, 15–16

Rubin, Andy, 73

Rubio, Jen, 38

Rule of 21, 109–111, 144

Rushdie, Salman, 28, 77

Ryan, Eric, 61–62

Ryan, Shawn, 29–30

S

Salesforce, 69

Schaller, George, 114

Schmidt, Eric, 100–101

Schwartz, Sam, 68–69, 141

Seinfeld, Jerry, 97–98, 143

self-awareness, 158–159

Sequoia Capital, 123

Sesame Workshop, 174

Sharkey, Tina, 62–63, 73, 174–182

The Shield (TV show), 29–30

Silicon Valley (TV show), 80–83
Simon & Schuster, 56–58
sincerity, 157–159
slides, 25–26
Smith, Brad, 206
social media, 177–179
Solivan, Leah, 108, 119
Sony Pictures Television, 65, 68
SoulCycle, 131
South by Southwest, 24
Spaly, Brian, 71
Spiridellis, Gregg, 119
Splash (film), 129
Stanton, Andrew, 99
Stein, Joel, 78–79, 91
Stern, Howard, 57–58, 140
Stewart, Jon, 103
storyboards, 39–43, 139
storytelling, 203–204
    bullet points vs., 26
    central characters for, 33–47
    facts and figures vs., 42–43
    heroes in, 85–90
    knowing your audience for,
        35–38
    multiple narratives in, 189–190
    Obama and, 111–113
    storyboards for, 39–43
    the story of us in, 82–85
Strauss, Neil, 104
student loan debt repayment,
    37–38
style, 15–16, 111–113, 144
subscriptions, 69–70
suitcase startups, 39
Sun Microsystems, 100–101
Superhuman, 42
sustainability, 166–167, 169–170,
    172–173

T
TaskRabbit, 108, 119
Taylor, Maureen, 100–101, 117
TED Talks, number one of all
    time, 16

themes, 193–199
"then what" exercise, 125–126
Thief Coach (film), 92–93
Thiel, Peter, 105
throwaway work, 28–30, 140,
    184–185
Thunberg, Greta, 131
time, for idea incubation, 18–23
Titanic (film), 51, 139–140, 155,
    159, 160–161
Tough Mudder, 27
transparency, 160
Trenchard, Bill, 42
trends, 150–151
    Method and, 167–169
    showing inevitability and,
        61–66
Trump, Donald, 133
truths, universal, 181–182
20th Century Fox, 155
Tzuo, Tien, 69

U
Uber, 45, 141
universal truths, 181–182
Upfront Ventures, 122–123
UserTesting.com, 48–49

V
Venkatesh, Sudhir, 51–52, 58
vision, 71–74, 141, 151, 189–190
    developing, 153–154
    sharing what it could be and,
        78–82
    visions vs., 201
Vohra, Rahul, 42

W
Walk, Hunter, 98, 101–102
Walmart, 70–71
Wasserman, Lew, 129
Waymo, 68
Weight Watchers, 59–60, 140
Weiss, Emily, 84–85
WeWork, 71–73

WhatsApp, 116–117
Wired magazine, 73
Wisconsin, in 2016 election, 54
Wizard of Oz (Baum), 86
Wood, Brian, 88–89, 142
Wu-Tang Clan, 197–198

X
The X-Files (TV show), 162, 163–164
Xfinity Mobile, 141

Y
Y Combinator, 19
Yung Skeeter. *See* McFedries, Trevor

Z
Zappos, 70–71
Zimride, 53–54. *See also* Lyft
Zuckerberg, Mark, 116
Zuora, 70

ABOUT THE AUTHORS

Suneel Gupta is the co-founder of Rise and teaches innovation at Harvard University. Using the seven steps inside this book, he went from being the face of failure for the *New York Times* to being the "New Face of Innovation" for the New York Stock Exchange. He also serves as an emissary for Gross National Happiness between the United States and the Kingdom of Bhutan. After nearly a decade of working with startups in San Francisco, Gupta moved back to his hometown in Michigan, where he lives with his wife, Leena, two daughters, Samara "Sammy" and Serena "Zuzu," and goldendoodle Noe.

Carlye Adler is an award-winning journalist and four-time *New York Times* bestselling coauthor-collaborator. She lives in Connecticut with her husband, two daughters, and skateboarding bulldog.